Peter Lucantoni

Introduction to

English as a Second Language

Teacher's Book

Revised Fourth Edition

CAMBRIDGE
UNIVERSITY PRESS

CAMBRIDGE
UNIVERSITY PRESS

University Printing House, Cambridge CB2 8BS, United Kingdom

Cambridge University Press is part of the University of Cambridge.

It furthers the University's mission by disseminating knowledge in the pursuit of education, learning and research at the highest international levels of excellence.

Information on this title: education.cambridge.org

First published 2015

Revised edition 2015
Reprinted 2015

Printed in the United Kingdom by Printondemand-worldwide, Peterborough

ISBN 978-1-107-53276-2 Paperback

Additional resources for this publication at education.cambridge.org

Contents

Introduction

This Teacher's Book supports the *Introduction to English as a Second Language*, Fourth edition. It is assumed that students following this course will not yet be in a position to focus on the IGCSE English as a Second Language examination itself.

The Teacher's Book provides the following:

- full guidance on how to approach all the tasks in the Coursebook
- suggestions for differentiated activities to use with mixed-ability classes
- answers to all the exercises in the Coursebook

The course provides students with a broad content-based Coursebook, exposing them to a wide variety of topics, themes and vocabulary, while at the same time consolidating essential language in the Use of English sections. Each of the 18 themed units is divided into sections, covering speaking and thinking skills, reading and vocabulary, writing, listening, use of English, and project work.

The Coursebook is divided into two parts: *The world around us* and *Human endeavour*. Each part is subdivided into units covering key questions such as How many planets are there in space?, What's an ecosystem?, Who was Ibn Battuta? and How much water do you use? Students are encouraged to learn for themselves through an inductive approach that encourages them to notice aspects of language in contextualised examples. While the book is content-based, it does not assume any previous knowledge of a particular subject. However, students are continually encouraged to work things out for themselves and to use alternative sources of information to find solutions to tasks and problems. For those in secondary or high-school contexts, they may be able to draw on other curriculum subjects.

Many units in the Coursebook contain information about learning skills. These are tips and strategies that students can apply during their learning to make it more effective. Also, every unit contains at least one Did You Know? box, which will provide students with some additional information on something they have read or heard about in the unit. Every unit also contains two Use of English sections, which highlight important areas of language and how it is used. Students are encouraged to notice examples of language in context (in the listening and reading texts) and use these as examples for their own language production, both spoken and written.

Many teachers will be working with mixed-ability groups of students. This Teacher's Book provides a variety of techniques that teachers can use to support weaker students and challenge stronger students. It may be useful to look through all the differentiated activities at the start of the course, to get an idea of the techniques suggested for various activities. Just because a differentiated activity appears in Unit 10 does not mean it cannot be applied to an activity earlier (or later) in the course.

For writing activities, no word limits are given as this will depend very much on your students' abilities. Remember that not all students need to be writing the same number of words in response to a writing task. If your students will eventually be taking the IGCSE English as a Second Language examination, the maximum number of words required is usually 150–200, so you can use this as a target for stronger students towards the end of this course. For this reason, 'sample' answers for writing tasks have not been provided.

Peter Lucantoni

Coursebook materials
UNIT 1: How many planets are there in space?

Unit introduction

Each unit begins with a brief overview of the topics and Use of English areas that students will read about. In this first unit, the topics are **space and space travel** and **the Hubble Space Telescope.** The Use of English areas are **passive verb forms,** *wh-* **question forms** and **time sequencers.**

A Speaking and thinking
(Coursebook pages 7–8)

1   Pairs
If you think that students will not know the names of many of the planets in English, you could immediately direct them to the image on page 7 and the anagrams in Activity A2. However, if they are happy to discuss the questions without too much support, give them a few minutes to do so, monitoring their discussions but not interfering. The aim is to introduce students to the unit topic and to give them some freedom to talk without fear of correction.

2   Pairs
Many students enjoy working with letters and doing puzzles, so this type of activity provides some variety and an opportunity for visual and kinaesthetic learners to do well. There are nine anagrams for students to unscramble. There is no reason why you should not give two or three examples if you feel students will struggle. Note that the names of the planets are always spelt with a capital first letter.
ANSWERS: **a** Neptune, **b** Jupiter, **c** Mercury, **d** Pluto, **e** Venus, **f** Saturn, **g** Mars, **h** Earth, **i** Uranus

3/4 Pairs
Activity A3 discusses where the different planets got their names from and asks students to think about the names of the planets in their own language. In Activity A4, students match the list of gods/goddesses to the planets. Once again, it does not matter if students do not have too much knowledge at this stage. Provide as much support as you think is necessary.

ANSWERS:

Position	Name	God/goddess
1	Mercury	winged messenger of the gods
2	Venus	goddess of love and beauty
3	Earth	
4	Mars	god of war
5	Jupiter	king of the gods
6	Saturn	god of farming and agriculture and father of Jupiter
7	Uranus	god of the sky and heavens and father of Saturn
8	Neptune	god of the sea
9	Pluto	god of the underworld

B Listening (Coursebook page 8)

1   Pairs
Give students time to think about the information in the table in their notebooks and to guess how the planets got their names. They will find the answers in the listening activity that follows. There is no need to provide any answers at this stage.

2   Alone, then pairs
Prepare students for the audio. Make sure they understand who they are going to hear talking (Taran), what the topic is going to be (how the planets got their names) and what they need to do (check if their ideas in Activity B1 were correct). When students are ready, play the audio once and then let students check their answers with a partner.

TRACK 2

Have you ever wondered how the planets got their names? I mean, why are they called Mercury and Uranus and Jupiter, and so on? Not exactly easy to remember, are they?

Well, all of the planets, except for Earth, are named after Greek and Roman gods and goddesses. Jupiter, Saturn, Mars, Venus and Mercury were given their names thousands of years ago, but nobody knows exactly when nor by whom.

The other planets – Uranus, Neptune and Pluto – were not discovered until much later, when telescopes were invented, and so their names were given more recently: Uranus in 1781, Neptune in 1846 and Pluto as recently as 1930. The tradition of naming the planets after Greek and Roman gods continued for these last three planets as well.

Going back to the oldest planets, Mercury, the winged messenger, was named after the Roman god of travel. The name was given because Mercury is the fastest planet – it completes one revolution around the sun in just 88 days. Venus was named after the Roman goddess of love and beauty because this planet appears as the brightest and most beautiful in the sky, after Earth's moon.

Some of you might know that Mars was the Roman god of war, but why was the name given to this planet? Well, Mars is red in colour and this colour was associated with blood in battles.

Jupiter got its name because it's the largest of all the planets – the king!

Saturn was the Roman god of agriculture, but it is not exactly clear how the planet got its name.

Uranus, the father of Saturn, is positioned next to it, and got its name from the ancient Greek god of the sky.

Neptune has a beautiful blue colour and so the Romans named it after their god of the sea.

Pluto, which is no longer classified as a planet, is the furthest from the sun and is always in darkness, just like the underworld, the place beneath the ground in mythology.

Our planet, Earth, is not named after a god or goddess – it's an English/German word which simply means 'the ground'. Boring, huh?!

3   Whole class, then alone, then pairs
It is a useful strategy to encourage students to think about the key word/s in questions, as this will help them to identify where to find the answers in a text (both listening and reading). It is also a good idea to get students to think about the **type** of answer each question is looking for, and to make possible predictions. For example question B3a asks *When were the planets Jupiter, Saturn, Mars, Venus and Mercury named?* The key words are *When, named* and *the planets*. *When* and *named* mean that students

need to listen for a date/year. The answer could be that Jupiter, Saturn, Mars, Venus and Mercury were all named at the same time (likely), or that there is a different date for each planet (unlikely, as this would mean listening for four different dates, and then writing them down before proceeding to the next question).

Students listen and write the answers in their notebooks, then check with a partner. The audioscript appears on page 150 of the Coursebook, so you can refer students to this as an additional (and student-centred) checking method.

ANSWERS:
a thousands of years ago
b (i) 1781, (ii) 1846, (iii) 1930
c Mercury
d blood in battles
e Jupiter
f because of its beautiful (sea) blue colour
g Pluto

C Use of English: Passive verbs
(Coursebook pages 9–10)

1/2 Alone, then whole class
Before beginning Activity C1, focus on the blue box about passive verbs and ask students to complete the rule: *The passive is formed with the verb **to be**, followed by the **past participle** of a main verb.*

Students start Activity C1 on their own, focusing on the underlined verbs in sentences a–c. All the verbs are in the passive form (voice).

For Activity C2, look at the first sentence together and explain to students who or what is the person or thing affected by the action (*all of the planets … are named* and *Jupiter, Mars, Venus and Mercury were given …*). The doer is not specified in either example here.

Then get students to look at sentences b and c and identify who or what is affected by each action, and to ask themselves who the doer is.

ANSWERS: b *this colour* was associated, **c** *Pluto* is no longer classified; we do not know who the doer is

3   Alone, then pairs
Give students a minute or so to complete a copy of the table in their notebooks, then get them to check with a partner.

ANSWERS:
were given = **past simple**
was associated = **past simple**
is classified = **present simple**

4 Pairs

Now that students know the pattern for forming passive verb forms, they should be able to find the answers here quite easily.

ANSWERS:

present perfect = *have/has been* + past participle
past perfect = *had been* + past participle

5 Pairs or whole class

Focus on the picture of the Hubble Space Telescope (HST) and ask students if they have ever heard of it and, if so, what they know about it. Discuss this as a class or split students into pairs to talk about it.

6 Alone, then pairs

Students work on their own and read the text. While they read, they should write the correct passive forms of the verbs in brackets in their notebooks, then check their answers with a partner.

ANSWERS:

a was launched
b have been delighted
c are used
d is hidden
e is slightly curved
f is made
g is turned
h are transmitted
i is sent
j is streamed
k are turned
l is collected
m is stored

D Reading (Coursebook pages 10–12)

1 Small groups

Put students into small groups in order to talk about questions a–d. There are no right or wrong answers, so encourage students to talk freely. You should not interfere, but monitor and provide support if required. Make sure you give positive feedback at the end of the discussions.

2/3 Small groups

Students continue their discussions by looking at the picture and answering the questions. Once again, it does not matter if they guess the answers incorrectly.

4 Pairs

Throughout the Coursebook, new words and phrases are introduced and it is often suggested that students use paper and/or digital reference sources

to make sure they understand this new vocabulary. You can ask the whole class to check all the words, or allocate different words to different students, depending on the amount of time available and how difficult you think they might find the words or phrases.

5 Alone, then pairs

Another recurring activity throughout the Coursebook asks students to think about vocabulary items in their own language and to provide a translation for an English word. In this way, they can build up their own bilingual dictionary. Encourage students to make a note of the grammar (part of speech) for new words and to add an example sentence so that new words are recorded in a meaningful context, as shown in the table on page 11. When students have completed their own table for this activity, get them to share their answers with a partner.

ANSWERS: ambitious = adjective, centrepiece = noun, daring = adjective or participle, habitable = adjective, manoeuvres = noun, obstacles = noun, severed = adjective or verb, withstand = verb, zap = verb

6/7 Alone, then pairs

Students read the text and check their answers to Activity D3. If you prefer, they could do Activity D7 at the same time. However, they should work alone and only pair up to check their answers once they have finished both activities.

ANSWERS (D6):

2 metres = arm
3 metres by 2.8 metres = length and width
2.1 metres = height
900 kilograms = weight
50.8 centimetre diameter = wheels

ANSWERS (D7): a centrepiece, **b** ambitious, **c** zap, **d** obstacles, **e** daring, **f** manoeuvres, **g** withstand, **h** altitude, **i** severed, **j** habitable

8 Alone, then pairs

Remind students to think about the key word/s in each question and to predict the type of answers required. They should work alone, then compare their answers with a partner.

ANSWERS:

a to find out if Mars is, or was, suitable for life and to learn more about the red planet's environment
b allows it to carry many scientific experiments
c a full Martian year is 687 Earth days
d from 26th November 2011 to 6th August 2012
e fiery
f a supersonic parachute, rockets, sky crane

3

E Use of English (Coursebook page 13)

Focus first on the blue box, which contains important information about *wh-* questions and the word order required for these.

1 Whole class, then pairs

Do the first example with the class, checking that they understand why *what* is the object of the question. Then in pairs students look at questions b–f, deciding if *who*, *what* or *which* is the subject or the object and answering the questions.

ANSWERS:

b *who* = subject, NASA
c *what* = subject, a supersonic parachute
d *who* = subject, NASA personnel
e *which* = subject, Twitter and Facebook
f *what* = subject, (various answers possible)

2 Whole class, then alone, then pairs

Look at the first part of this question (a) with the class and check that students understand what they have to do. Then students write their answers and check them with a partner.

ANSWERS:

b Who designed the assembly to *roll over obstacles*?
c What severed *the link*?
d What was *used for the final part of the landing sequence*?
e *What is* Curiosity's *main mission*?
f *How did scientists feel when the rover beamed back information*?

F Writing (Coursebook pages 13–14)

1 Whole class, then pairs

Go through the expressions from the unit texts that describe **when** something happened. Make sure students understand that using phrases, rather than individual words, can make their writing more effective and interesting. Then, in pairs, students look again at the *Mars* Curiosity text and find more examples of time sequencers.

ANSWERS: On 26th November 2011, on 6th August 2012, Firstly, Then, When

2/3 Alone

Students build up information about space achievements by looking back at the texts in the unit and selecting at least four more important events to add to the ones in Activity F2. This will give them a total of nine or ten pieces of information, which they should combine into a paragraph, using time sequencers as appropriate.

4 Alone

For this activity, students use the notes given to write a paragraph about missions into space.

SAMPLE ANSWER:

During the early 1960s, many attempts were made by the USSR to reach Mars, but all ended in failure for a variety of reasons. The first success was in 1964, when the USA's *Mariner 4* sent back 21 images. During the late 1960s there were more attempts by the USSR, but none was successful because of launch failures. Then, in 1971, the USSR had its first success when the *Mars 3* Orbiter-Lander sent back data for eight months. It landed on Mars, but only sent 20 seconds of data. In the mid-1970s, the US *Viking 1* and *2* Orbiter-Lander returned 1600 images and a large quantity of data and soil experiments. However, for the next 20 years there were mostly failures from the USA, USSR and China. In 1985, Sultan bin Salman Al Saud joined the international crew on *Discovery* and launched a satellite into space. In the early to mid 2000s, there was plenty of USA success, with enormous amounts of data being sent back. In 2012, Chinese astronauts ate fresh vegetables from gardens in extra-terrestrial bases in space.

DIFFERENTIATED ACTIVITY

For weaker students, offer more support in this writing section. For Activities F2 and F3, they could use just the notes in the Coursebook, rather than finding extra ones to make a longer list. You could allocate two or three of the notes to different students to complete, and then students join their sentences together to make a complete paragraph. In Activity F4, you could complete more notes for them (perhaps a, c, e and g), then students have to complete the others and thus create the whole paragraph. In addition, you could put the verbs into the correct tenses for them.

For stronger students, encourage them to expand on the notes as much as possible by using more descriptive language (adverbs and adjectives). Another variation could be for students to write their paragraph, then turn the content into a question-and-answer interview. For example the first question might be: *Tell us about the early attempts to reach Mars*, with the answer: *During the early 1960s, many attempts were made by the USSR to reach Mars, but all ended in failure for a variety of reasons.* The next question might be *When did the first success happen?* with the answer *The first success was in 1964 when the USA's* Mariner 4 *sent back 21 images*, and so on.

G Project work (Coursebook page 14)

Every unit in the Coursebook concludes with a section on project work. The idea is for students to work independently if possible, and to expand on the knowledge that they have acquired from the unit. The project can be done at home, at school, or a combination of both, depending on the resources available to students. The time required for students to complete the project will vary. The important thing is for students to create something (in this unit, it is an illustrated classroom poster) and be ready to present their work to the class and answer any questions.

Coursebook materials
UNIT 2: What's a living creature?

Unit introduction

In this unit, the topics are **natural history**, **living things** and **turtles**, and the Use of English areas are **adverbs**, **word building** and **'signpost'** words.

A Speaking and thinking
(Coursebook pages 15–16)

1 **Whole class, then pairs**
Check that students understand what a museum of natural history will contain, then get them to focus on the six pieces of information (a–f). Help them with any difficult vocabulary. Students then decide with their partners if the information is true or false. There is no need to tell them if they are right or wrong, as they will find out for themselves in the next activity.

2 **Alone**
Students quickly read the paragraph to check their answers to Activity A1 (everything is true).

3 **Whole class, then pairs**
The eight pictures show things that can be seen in the Natural History Museum. Let students tell you as much as they can about each picture, allowing them the freedom to get things wrong at this stage. Then refer them to the list of names on the next page to see if they can match them correctly to the pictures.

ANSWERS: 1g, 2e, 3c, 4b, 5f, 6h, 7a, 8d

4 **Pairs**
Ask students what they would like to see in the museum. Would it be something from the list in Activity A3, or something that is not mentioned? Get them to talk together and to give reasons for their choices.

B Listening (Coursebook pages 16–17)

1/2 **Whole class, then pairs**
Prepare students for the audio by checking that they understand who they are going to listen to (a Natural History Museum volunteer) and what they are going to talk about (the most amazing thing in the museum). Also make sure they understand that this is an interview, not a monologue, so they can expect to hear a series of questions with answers. Before students listen, get them to work with a partner and check the meaning of the words in the box, using paper or digital reference sources. For Activity B2, ask them to guess which animal the volunteer is going to talk about.

3 **Whole class, then pairs**
Go through the numbers in the box, getting students to say each number aloud. This will help them to recognise the numbers when they hear them during the listening activity. Students should also look at statements a–e and guess which numbers are appropriate to complete the information.

ANSWERS: a 2.5 metres, b 500 kilograms, c 2200 metres, d 30–40 centimetres, e 8.62 metres

4 **Alone, then pairs**
Students listen and check their answers to Activities B2 and B3.

TRACK 3

Jonathan: Last week I interviewed Caroline Foster, a volunteer at the Natural History Museum in London. Here's what happened … Thanks for talking to me, Caroline.

Caroline Foster: Hello, Jonathan.

J: Caroline, what do you think is the most amazing thing in the museum's collection?

C: That's a very difficult question to answer, as the whole place is just so incredible! But I think, if I had to choose one thing, it would be the colossal squid.

J: Colossal means enormous, doesn't it?

C: Yes, and the name is very appropriate! The specimen was caught in 2005 off the South Georgia islands in the South Atlantic and it was generously donated to the museum by the British Antarctic Survey. When the squid arrived here, it was preserved and prepared for display.

J: So, how enormous is it?

C: Well, this juvenile squid is approximately 2.5 metres long and includes arms, one tentacle and the head.

J: Really? But some of it is definitely missing, right?

C: Unfortunately, yes, quite a lot of the squid is missing. It would have been much longer, maybe over 5 metres, if it had had its body, as this takes up half of the squid's length. Imagine, a specimen was caught in 2007 which weighed nearly 500 kilograms! The colossal squid is possibly the largest living invertebrate and we think it reaches larger sizes than the giant squid. Despite its size and weight, it can move incredibly fast.

J: OK, but why don't you know for sure?

C: It's really quite simple: a fully grown specimen has, so far, never been found.

J: Why not?

C: Because they live in the deep ocean at depths of at least 2200 metres, and this is the main reason why finding specimens is so hard. Very little is known about them and what scientists do know often comes from the remains of dead or dying specimens.

J: So what do we know about this monster squid?

C: Well, the colossal squid has the largest eyes of any known living animal, between 30 and 40 centimetres. Their eyes face forward, unlike the giant squid's. Strangely, their eyes are on the side of the head.

J: Incredible! What else?

C: Believe it or not, the colossal squid has an impressive three hearts, which have different functions. One heart constantly pumps blood to the gills, where oxygen is taken up. Blood then flows to another heart, where it is pumped to the rest of the body. Squid blood is blue, not red as in humans. You can see the colossal squid, along with the museum's 8.62 metres giant squid 'Archie', when you book onto a free Spirit Collection Tour.

J: Spirit Collection Tour? What's that, exactly?

C: Well, these tours give visitors a glimpse of some of the 27 kilometres of shelves …

J: Excuse me, did you say 27 kilometres of shelves?

C: Yes, incredible, isn't it? 27 kilometres of shelves of preserved specimens, such as huge fish, reptiles, deep-sea invertebrates and other material. Visitors can also find out about the scientific work that goes on behind the scenes.

J: So what type of scientific work is done at the museum?

C: Well, having complete specimens is really extremely important as it allows scientists to learn much more about the animal, from obvious things, such as what it looks like, to what it eats by looking in its stomach.

J: I see.

C: DNA from the museum's giant squid was sent for analysis. Scientists hope to find out information, such as how closely related it is to other squid species and if there is more than one giant squid species worldwide.

J: We think of a museum as full of dead things, but in fact museums are alive and kicking! Thank you Caroline for that fascinating insight in the Natural History Museum. Now, …

Adapted from www.nhm.ac.uk

5 **Whole class, then alone, then pairs**
Quickly check that there are no vocabulary problems with the questions a–h. Students then listen again and write the answers in their notebooks. They can check their answers with a partner afterwards.

ANSWERS:
a it was donated/a donation
b quite a lot/its body/tentacles
c a fully grown specimen has never been found
d colossal squid's eyes face forward, giant squid's eyes on side of head
e on the Spirit Collection Tour
f huge fish, reptiles, deep-sea invertebrates
g scientists can learn much more if specimens are complete
h how closely related it is to other species, and if there is more than one giant squid species

6 **Pairs**
Students work together to try to recreate part of the interview they have just listened to. They need to look at seven of Jonathan's questions and supply Caroline's answers. They can use the audioscript on pages 150–1 to check.

ANSWERS:
a That's a very difficult question to answer
b Well, the juvenile squid …
c Unfortunately, yes, quite a lot …
d It's really quite simple …
e Well, the colossal squid …
f Yes, incredible, isn't it?
g Well, having complete specimens …

7

DIFFERENTIATED ACTIVITY

For weaker students, allow them to look at the audioscript **before** they listen, to give them an idea of the content and build up their confidence before they listen. They could also read the audioscript **while** they listen. A third option (offering a bit less support) is to allow students to read the audioscript **after** they have listened as a way of confirming their understanding. Remember that reading the audioscript is **not** a class activity in this case – it is done solely to provide support for weaker students. You could supply key words or prompts for the questions in Activity B5. For Activity B6, you could give them all of Caroline's answers and ask students to match them to the questions.

For stronger students, get them to write the questions in Activity B5 from prompts. They should work with their books closed while you give them key words to create the questions. For example question a: *How / NHM / get / colossal squid specimen?*, question b: *What / miss / from / squid specimen?*, question c: *Why / scientists / unsure / exact size / colossal squid?* etc. You could use a similar approach in Activity B6, supplying key words for Jonathan's questions for students to remember Caroline's answers.

LEARNING SKILLS

Learning skills boxes appear throughout the Coursebook. These contain effective learning strategies that students can use. Go through each one as they appear in the units, checking that they understand the strategy and making sure they appreciate how useful it could be in their learning.

C Use of English: Adverbs
(Coursebook pages 17–18)

1 Alone, then pairs
Get students to focus on the information about adverbs in the green box, then look at the sentences taken from the listening activity in the previous section. Each sentence contains an adverb, which students first need to identify and then decide whether it is modifying a verb, an adjective, another adverb or a phrase. They should work alone, then check their answers with a partner.

ANSWERS: **a** verb, **b** adverb, **c** phrase, **d** phrase, **e** adjective

2 Alone, then pairs
Students need to unjumble the sentences and write them out in their notebooks, making sure that they position the underlined adverbs in the correct place. They should also decide if each adverb is modifying a verb, an adjective, another adverb or a phrase. They can compare answers with a partner and also look again at the audioscript on page 150–1 if they need to.

ANSWERS:
a That's a <u>very</u> difficult question to answer (adjective)
b It was <u>generously</u> donated (verb)
c <u>Strangely</u>, their eyes are on the side of the head (phrase)
d One heart <u>constantly</u> pumps blood (verb)
e Having complete specimens is <u>really</u> <u>extremely</u> important (adverb/adjective)

3 Pairs
Students try to identify the creatures in the pictures and say if any of them live in their country. Do not correct students, as they will find out more in the following activities.

4 Pairs
The words in the box do not match the pictures in Activity C3 – these creatures appear in the text that follows. Students need to have an idea of what they are, so give them some time to use paper and digital reference sources to check.

5 Alone
Students work alone to identify in the text the five animals in the pictures in Activity C3. They do not need to worry about the gaps at the moment.

ANSWERS: 1 = snake (saw-scaled viper), 2 = bat (Sind Batina Serotine), 3 = (Arabian) oryx, 4 = gazelle, 5 = hare

6 Alone, then pairs
Students work on their own and read the text in more detail. While they read, they should complete the gaps a–n with an appropriate adverb. A choice of adverbs is given at the end of each paragraph, but there is one extra adverb for each paragraph that students do not need to use – make sure they understand this. Students write their answers in their notebooks, and then check with their partner.

ANSWERS: **a** apparently, **b** recently, **c** suddenly, **d** completely, **e** extremely, **f** finally, **g** virtually, **h** incredibly, **i** apparently, **j** safely, **k** successfully, **l** totally, **m** Amazingly, **n** eventually

D Reading (Coursebook pages 19–20)

1/2 Pairs, then whole class

There is some quite challenging vocabulary in the text in this section, much of it scientific, but as many students will have studied science at school some of the vocabulary may already be familiar. Give students some time to use paper or digital reference sources to check the meaning of the 12 words in the box in Activity D1. If you prefer, you could allocate different words to different students so that not all students have to work on all 12 words. Do class feedback to check that everyone understands the words. Afterwards, go through the information in Activity D2 carefully, before students work in pairs to check the meaning of the seven basic characteristics of living things.

3 Alone, then pairs

Students now skim the text and match the paragraphs to the characteristics in Activity D2.

ANSWERS: 1 = nutrition, 2 = reproduction, 3 = movement, 4 = respiration, 5 = excretion, 6 = growth, 7 = sensitivity

4 Whole class, then alone, then pairs

Go through questions a–g with students, reminding them to look for key word/s and to think about the type of answer each question requires. Check any difficult vocabulary. Students then write the answers in their notebooks before comparing with a partner.

ANSWERS:

a to gain energy, to make new cells and to stay healthy
b it grows into a new plant
c it can move substances from one part of the body to another part
d to breathe and to produce energy
e waste could become toxic/dangerous
f by growth of cells and adding new cells
g respond/react

E Use of English: Word building
(Coursebook pages 20–1)

1/2 Whole class, then alone, then pairs

Focus on the blue box first of all, showing students how we can form different parts of speech and change meanings by adding prefixes or suffixes (and sometimes both) to a word. Then students work on their own to copy and complete the table. Do some examples first. When students have completed as much as they can, they can look back at the text and

add three or four more words to their table. They can check their answers with a partner and decide on the best noun equivalent in their own language.

ANSWERS:

Verb	Noun	Adjective	Adverb
	health	healthy	healthily
fertilise	fertility	fertile/fertilised	
produce	product/production/producer	produced	
move	movement/mover	moved	
energise	energy	energetic	energetically
respond	response	responsive	responsively
protect	protection/protector	protected/protective	protectively

> **LANGUAGE TIP**
> 'Signpost' words
> Make sure you go through the information on signpost words with students, then get them to copy and complete the table, which they can add to as they work through the Coursebook.

F Writing (Coursebook pages 21–2)

1 Pairs

The five pictures show the life cycle of a sea turtle. Students work together to decide on the correct order for the pictures. They should discuss what they think happens at each stage in the cycle.

2/3 Pairs

Working together, students check the meaning of the nine words and phrases in the box and match them to the five pictures. Then they describe the life cycle of the sea turtle again, making any adjustments necessary and using the words and phrases in the box. When they have finished, students should read the text on page 22 and check how well they described the life cycle.

4 Alone

Students read the text again and answer questions a–c.

ANSWERS: a 1, b 2/3, c 3/4/5

5 Alone, then pairs

This is a 'reverse dictionary' activity. Students work on their own to find eight words in the text that have a similar meaning to the words and phrases given. When they have found all the words, they can check with their partner. If you think eight words is too many for students to find, divide the words and phrases up between students.

ANSWERS: a breathtaking, **b** mass, **c** emerging, **d** endangered, **e** conceal, **f** phenomena, **g** wiped out, **h** predators

6 Alone

Students now have a lot of information and relevant vocabulary about sea turtles, and they have already described their life cycle. Now they need to put everything together and write four or five sentences, beginning each sentence with an appropriate 'signpost' word.

G Project work (Coursebook page 22)

Spend some time ensuring that students understand what they have to do for this project, which has two stages. Firstly they need to copy and complete the table, then use this to design an information leaflet.

Coursebook materials
UNIT 3: What's a hurricane?

Unit introduction

In this unit, the topics are **the weather, natural disasters** and **Pompeii**, and the Use of English areas are **abstract nouns**, **conditionals** and *if only*.

A Speaking and thinking
(Coursebook page 23)

1/2 Alone, pairs or whole class
If students do not have easy access to the Internet or reference books, you could supply pictures for the first activity and get students to match them to the 11 events listed. Find out what relevant vocabulary or phrases students know by asking them to tell you some of the characteristics. For example volcano = ash, lava, eruption, hailstorm = frozen rain, shaped like small balls, etc. Get them to work with a partner to copy and complete the table.

ANSWERS:
Violent weather: hailstorm, flood, drought, hurricane, tornado, sandstorm
Violent Earth: volcano, avalanche, mudslide, earthquake, tsunami

3 Pairs
Students focus on the diagram of the formation of a hurricane and describe what happens. They should use the notes in the diagram, and link the stages together using 'signpost' words.

4 Pairs
Students read the three statements about hurricanes and decide if the information is true or false. There is no need to tell them yet if they are right or wrong, as they will find out in the next section.

B Listening (Coursebook pages 24–5)

1 Pairs
Before students listen to John Devonport, a meteorologist, they should work with a partner on the vocabulary activities a–d.

In activity a, encourage students to draw a diagram such as a mind map, as this is a good way to record thematic vocabulary. For example:

b Students decide which words in the box have a similar meaning to *big*.
ANSWERS: huge, enormous, large, massive, gigantic

c Students match the verbs with an appropriate meaning
ANSWERS: spiral + go around and around, lasts + continues for a period of time, gather + collect, rotate + turn, occur + happen

d There are six words that students need to check, using paper or digital reference sources. They should find an equivalent word in their own language and add it to their bilingual dictionary.

2 Alone
Prepare students for the audio. Check that they understand who they are going to listen to (John Devonport, a meteorologist) and what he is going to be talking about (hurricanes). They then listen out for any of the words or phrases they thought of in Activity B1a, and decide how he feels about the subject of hurricanes, giving their reasons.

TRACK 3

Hello and welcome! My name is John Devonport and today I'm going to talk about hurricanes.

A hurricane is a huge storm, much stronger than the storms most people experience! It can be up to 1000 kilometres across and have strong winds which spiral in and up to speeds of 100 kilometres per hour. Sometimes the movement of the winds is even faster, at up to 300 kilometres per hour. Each hurricane usually lasts for over a week, moving about 15–30 kilometres per hour over the open sea. Hurricanes gather heat and energy as they make contact with warm waters, and evaporation from the seawater makes them more powerful. In the Northern Hemisphere, hurricanes rotate in an anticlockwise direction around an 'eye' (the centre of the storm), and in the Southern Hemisphere they rotate in a clockwise direction. The 'eye' is calm, with light winds and fair weather. When a hurricane comes on to land, the heavy rain, strong winds and large waves often damage buildings, trees and cars.

If you live in an area where hurricanes happen often, then an emergency hurricane kit, similar to the one in the picture, can be a big help for you. A hurricane survival kit is designed to give you all the basic things you need to survive and be safe, from how to get clean water for yourself to first-aid kits and other helpful tools.

A storm surge is frequently the most destructive element of a hurricane. As a hurricane's winds spiral around the storm, they push water into the storm's centre. This water becomes more dangerous when the storm reaches land because it can cause a flood along the coast. The water builds up, unable to escape anywhere but on to the land, as the storm pushes it harder and harder.

The Atlantic hurricane season is from 1st June to 30th November, but most hurricanes occur during the autumn months. The Eastern Pacific hurricane season is from 15th May to 30th November. Have a look at the map that shows you when hurricanes are most active across different parts of the world.

Many people ask me what the difference is between a hurricane, a cyclone and a typhoon, and the answer is very simple: there is no difference, except geography! They are all tropical storms and these happen in several of the world's oceans and, except for their names, they are all similar to each other. In the Atlantic Ocean, the Gulf of Mexico and the Eastern Pacific Ocean, they are called hurricanes. In the Western Pacific Ocean, they are called typhoons. In the Indian Ocean, the Bay of Bengal and Australia, these types of storms are called cyclones.

Adapted from www.weatherwizkids.com

3   **Alone, then pairs**
Students listen a second time and complete the notes. Then they can check with a partner and/or with the audioscript on page 151.
ANSWERS: a 1000, **b** 100, **c** 300, **d** 15, **e** 30, **f** evaporation (from seawater), **g** anticlockwise, **h** flood (along the coast), **i** 15th May, **j** 30th November, **k** hurricanes, **l** cyclones

4   **Pairs**
You could use a class wall map for this activity. Students need to find the places a–g on the map and decide if hurricanes, tornadoes or cyclones happen in each one.
ANSWERS:
Atlantic Ocean, Gulf of Mexico and the Eastern Pacific Ocean = hurricanes
Western Pacific Ocean = typhoons
Indian Ocean, Bay of Bengal, Australia = cyclones

C Use of English: Abstract nouns (Coursebook pages 25–6)

1   **Whole class, then alone**
Go through the information about abstract nouns in the blue box, then get students make five abstract nouns from the root words in the box on page 26. All the words appeared in the listening activity.
ANSWERS: movement, evaporation, direction, survival, difference

2   **Whole class**
Students need to decide which of the nouns in the box are abstract nouns. There is a large number of words, so you could allocate one or two columns to different groups of students, or allocate words by their initial letter, and so on.
ANSWERS: The following nouns are **not** abstract: apple, beach, book, computer, house, hurricane, injection, library, music, news, piano, planet, screen, shoe, table, telephone, traffic, wallet

3   **Whole class, then alone**
Make sure students understand what they have to do in this activity (i.e. write a poem). Read the example

with them and explain that they can write whatever they feel about their chosen abstract noun. Here is another example:

Love is definitely pink
It smells like fresh roses
It tastes like delicious chocolate
It sounds like cats playing
It feels like a soft new toy
It lives everywhere around us

D Reading (Coursebook pages 26–7)

1   Pairs
Many students may not have much experience of snow. Get them to think about what snow is and to write down any words or phrases that come to mind.

2/3 Pairs, then whole class
In these two activities, students need to check the meaning of weather-related vocabulary. Allow them to use paper or digital reference sources to do this, then collate class feedback. Students could use pictures or diagrams to demonstrate the meaning of some items.

4   Pairs
Students match the five pictures to a word or phrase in the *Safety tips* text.

ANSWERS: 1 = a long stick, 2 = a small spade,
3 = single file, 4 = personal tracking device,
5 = an anchor

E Use of English: Conditionals and *if only* (Coursebook pages 27–8)

1/2 Pairs
Focus on the information about conditionals and *if only* in the green box, checking that students understand what they have to do in Activities E1 and E2. Then get them to carry out the activities.

ANSWERS (BOX):
If you are in an avalanche area, take notice of warning signs.
If you are in an avalanche area, always carry safety equipment ...
If you are caught in the path of an avalanche, try to get to the side of it.
If you can't do this, hold on to an anchor, such as a tree.
If you are hit by an avalanche, 'swim' with the snow ...

ANSWERS (1): the verbs in the *if* clauses are present tense and those in the main clauses are all present tense without a subject = imperative forms. Where further advice is given in a second sentence, the imperative is used again (*Stay alert in the countryside ...*).

ANSWERS (2): this conditional form is used to do both b and c, although in the examples so far the meaning is for instructions, warnings, advice, suggestions.

3   Alone, then pairs
Students think of advice or suggestions for each of the situations about extreme weather. Focus on the example first to make sure students understand what they have to do. They should then write their answers and share them with a partner.

POSSIBLE ANSWERS:
a *If you have an emergency radio,* keep it turned on.
b *If you don't have a basement,* stay in the bathroom.
c *If you know a hurricane is coming,* keep the windows shuttered.
d *If you live in a hurricane area,* buy a power generator.
e *If you live in a mobile home,* move out when a hurricane approaches.
f *If you live on a boat,* don't stay on it.
g *If you see broken power cables,* don't go near them.

4   Whole class, then alone
Go through the information in the reading text, pointing out the use of the imperative form (infinitive verb without *to*) for giving advice or an instruction in a single clause: *Take notice of warning signs*. Also point out the use of *always* when we want to strengthen a piece of advice or an instruction: *Always take notice of warning signs*. Then students work on their own to answer questions a–c.

ANSWERS:
a keep away, wait, go, do, stay
b never, do not
c various answers possible

5   Whole class, then alone
Focus on the information about conditional structures that refer to the past, and the use of *If only* + past perfect to express past regret. The underlined verbs are either in the past perfect (*had* + past participle) or conditional perfect (modal + present perfect).

ANSWERS:
had taken = past perfect
wouldn't have gone = conditional perfect
hadn't walked = past perfect
would have been = conditional perfect

6   Alone
Students look back at the advice and suggestions they gave in Activity E4c, then change the advice to an expression of regret using *If only* + past perfect.

13

F Writing and reading
(Coursebook pages 28–30)

1 Pairs

Students look at the picture on page 29 and discuss what they can see, where it is and what they think happened. Allow them freedom to express their ideas, even if their guesses about the picture are incorrect.

2 Pairs

There is quite a lot of vocabulary in the box, so you may prefer to allocate words to different students in order to save time. Then all the answers can be shared. Students also need to choose ten of the words that they think will appear in the text about Pompeii.

3 Alone

Students have a quick look at the text and find and write down the words from Activity F2.

4 Whole class, then alone

Check that students understand that the short text is part of one of Pliny's letters (who they read about in the previous text about Pompeii). Students need to imagine that they are Pliny and describe what happened 'when it became dark'. They should use the prompts to help with their story:

When it became dark, who was with you? Friends?
Family?
Where were you exactly? Outside or inside?
What did you say to each other?
Did you give each other any advice?
How did you survive?
Do you have any regrets about what you did?

G Project work (Coursebook page 30)

There are three stages to this project. Firstly, students need to think about the weather in their own country, and find out how to describe the weather in their own language. Next, they do some research in order to complete the table. Finally, they produce a presentation for the class.

Unit introduction

In this unit, the topics are **water**, **sea monsters and dinosaurs** and **temperatures**, and the Use of English areas are **prepositional verbs**, **past simple** and **past perfect**.

A Speaking and thinking

(Coursebook pages 31–2)

1 **Alone or pairs**
   If students answer the five crossword clues correctly, another word will be revealed.
   ANSWERS: a shallow, **b** surface, **c** depth, **d** seaweed, **e** frozen (OCEAN)

2 **Pairs**
   Students use the five words from Activity A1 to complete the sentences, then decide if each one is true or false.
   ANSWERS: a surface, **d** depth, **f** seaweed / shallow, **g** frozen
   a true, **b** true, **c** true, **d** false, **e** false, **f** true, **g** true, **h** true

3/4 **Whole class, then pairs**
   Focus on the eight pictures, which students need to match with the correct names from the list a–h, then with the correct height or depth from Activity A4. First, go through the names and heights and depths, checking that students know how to say them. Give students plenty of time to think about all the information given, and encourage them to discuss their thoughts freely before they write down their answers.
   ANSWERS (3): 1 = g, 2 = e, 3 = a, 4 = b, 5 = h, 6 = c, 7 = f, 8 = d
   ANSWERS (4): 1 = 2313 metres, 2 = 300 metres, 3 = 8850 metres, 4 = 6887 metres, 5 = 2.51 metres, 6 = 2734 metres, 7 = 2191 metres, 8 = 4572 metres

5 **Alone**
   Once students have checked their answers with you, they should produce a graph or chart showing the various heights and depths. They could do this as a bar graph or a line graph similar to the ones below.

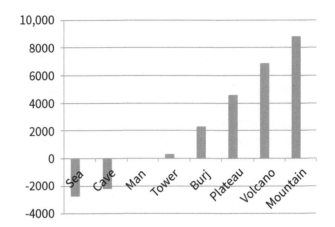

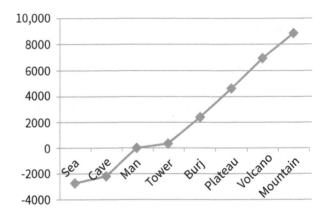

B Reading (Coursebook page 33–4)

1 **Whole class, then pairs**
   Tell the class that the world's deepest ocean (the Pacific Ocean, 10,294 metres) is more than 2000 metres deeper than the world's tallest mountain is high (on their graph they should see that Everest is 8850 metres). Ask them to show you on their graphs two things that have similar measurements above and below ground (Arabian Sea at 2734 metres deep and Burj Khalifa at 2313 metres high). Then ask for something that is twice the height of something else (Everest 8850 metres and Antarctic Plateau at 4572 metres).
   Focus on the table and point out that when we describe Earth, we sometimes use very large numbers that can contain many zeros. Students work together and complete as much of the table as they can.

ANSWERS: a hundred, **b** 1000, **c** six, **d** million, **e** 1000000000000, **f** 12, **g** trillion, **h** 1000000000000000, **i** 1000000000000000000, **j** 18, **k** quintillion

2   Pairs
Students work in pairs to check the meaning of the words in the box.

3   Alone, then pairs
Students skim through the text on page 34 and decide on a suitable heading for each paragraph. You could do the first one as an example, then let students work alone or in pairs to find headings for paragraphs 2–4. They should not worry about the gaps in the text or the phrases printed in blue for the moment.

4   Alone, then pairs
Students skim the text again, this time filling in the gaps with the words from Activity B2. When they have finished, get students to check their answers with a partner.
ANSWERS: a saline, **b** continuous, **c** gigantic, **d** descending, **e** equator, **f** portions, **g** evaporation, **h** evolved

5   Alone, then pairs
Numbers, especially longer ones, can be quite confusing and difficult for students to write in figures. In this activity, they focus on the phrases in blue, which all contain numbers. Students should write these as figures, including the measurement when given. They can check their answers with a partner.
ANSWERS: 35 parts per (or /) 1000, 70%, 361,000,000 square kilometres, 70%, 3,000,000,000 years

C   Use of English: Prepositional verbs (Coursebook pages 34–5)

1   Whole class, then alone
Focus on the information in the green box to make sure students understand what prepositional verbs are and how they are used. Then ask students to re-read the text on page 34 and try to find more examples of prepositional verbs.
ANSWERS: *split up*, *connected with* and *covered by*

2   Pairs
Sometimes a verb can be followed by different prepositions, with a change in meaning depending on where and how it is used. In pairs, students look at examples a and b and answer the questions.
ANSWERS: a person, **b** idea

3   Alone
Students write two sentences for each of the prepositional verbs from Activity C1: *split up*, *connected with* and *covered by.*

D   Listening (Coursebook pages 35–6)

1   Pairs or small groups
Students can discuss this question in pairs or small groups. Alternatively, you could open it up to the whole class. Make sure that you monitor discussions but do not interfere. Be ready to provide support if needed. Give positive comments during class feedback, and focus on any language areas that you feel need attention.

2   Pairs
Students work in pairs to check the meaning of the 12 words in the box.

3   Alone, then pairs
Prepare students for the audio by making sure they understand who they are going to be listening to (a marine biologist). As they listen, they should number the words from Activity D2 in the order that they hear them. They can check with a partner afterwards.

TRACK 5

About 250 to 60 million years ago, during the age of the dinosaurs, the earth was ruled by large reptiles and tiny mammals. This was during the Triassic and Jurassic periods. The dinosaurs lived on the land, but they also roamed the open oceans and inland seas.

By the end of the Triassic period, however, from about 200 million years ago, many of these sea monsters had become extinct and dinosaurs had begun to dominate the planet. The continents joined into one super-continent called Pangaea, but then this new continent split apart again before the end of the Triassic period, changing Earth's geography and climate.

The Jurassic period, from 200 million to 145 million years ago, was a very fertile and green period, during which giant grass-eating, or herbivorous, dinosaurs thrived. Smaller meat-eating, or carnivorous, animals also increased. The first birds appeared in the skies, and flowering plants and insects established themselves. The shallow seas filled with reefs, sharks and plesiosaurs.

The Jurassic period was followed by the Early Cretaceous period, until around 83 million years ago. The continents continued to move and separate and, by the end of this period, they resembled Earth's modern continents.

Between 83 and 65 million years ago, during the Late Cretaceous period, many animals had started to die out and, by the end of the period, there was a mass extinction, caused by the impact of an enormous asteroid, according to some scientists. Following this, the age of mammals began, which has continued up to the present day. Many mountain ranges have been formed during this time, including the Alps and the Rockies.

Adapted from www.nationalgeographic.com

ANSWERS: 1 reptiles, **2** mammals, **3** extinct, **4** fertile, **5** herbivorous, **6** thrived, **7** carnivorous, **8** insects, **9** reefs, **10** continents, **11** mass, **12** asteroid

4/5 Pairs
Students work together to complete the table, using the words from the box. Then they listen again and/or read the audioscript on page 151 to check their answers.

ANSWERS: a extinct, **b** climate, **c** dinosaurs, **d** carnivorous, **e** birds, **f** shallow, **g** separated, **h** geography, **i** animals, **j** extinction, **k** mammals, **l** mountain

DIFFERENTIATED ACTIVITY

For weaker students, tell them which words should be used in each of the four columns, thus making the selection of the correct words less challenging.

For stronger students, give them a copy of the gapped table to complete **without** the list of missing words. They need to remember what information goes into each gap.

E Use of English: Past simple and past perfect
(Coursebook pages 36–7)

1 Whole class, then pairs
Focus on the information in the green box, then explain to students that they need to fill in the gaps in the three paragraphs from the listening text, using the verbs from the box in the correct tense. Also point out that some of the verbs may need to be in the passive form.

ANSWERS: a joined, **b** split, **c** was, **d** thrived, **e** increased, **f** appeared, **g** established, **h** filled, **i** was followed, **j** continued, **k** resembled

F Speaking, reading and writing **(Coursebook pages 37–8)**

1/2 Pairs
Students discuss the word *hot* with their partner and try to agree on a meaning. They should then match the different possible meanings in the table.

ANSWERS:

A	B
His shirt was hot pink with blue spots.	bright, vivid colour
I think that topic is too hot to discuss.	something that causes an argument
Listen to this news hot off the press!	recent or topical
Martha has a very hot temper.	quickly angered
Petros is really hot on jazz.	keen, eager
That curry was too hot for me.	very spicy
The competition was too hot for our team.	knowledgeable
It's the hottest day of the year.	very warm
The protest got too hot and he left quickly.	dangerous
This car is the hottest in our range.	successful

3 Pairs
Now students turn their attention to the word *cold* and think of its different meanings. They should come up with their own ideas first, then use a dictionary to add to their list.

4/5 Pairs
Students discuss where they think the hottest and coldest places on Earth are. They should talk about the hottest and coldest places they have been to and whether they prefer to be in a hot or cold place.

6 Pairs
This is an information gap activity, in which pairs of students have access to different pieces of information. In this case, Student A is going to read a text about the hottest place on Earth, while Student B reads about the coldest place on Earth. Both texts

are on page 38, but one text is upside down, so students only read their own text.

After students have read their text, they ask each other questions to obtain the information required. They should make a note of the answers, then write a paragraph using the information. Finally, they read their partner's text to check that they have correctly noted all the important facts.

ANSWERS:

	Hottest place/s	Coldest place/s
Name	1 Dallol Depression 2 Death Valley	Antarctica
Location	1 Ethiopia 2 California, USA	Antarctica
Temperature	1 63 °C in the sun 2 49 °C in the sun	−89 °C
Geographical features	1 desert, some places 100 m below sea level, one of lowest places on Earth not covered by water 2 miles of sand dunes, salt lake, mountains, volcanic rock	one of driest places on Earth, sun rises and sets only once a year – six months of darkness and six months of daylight
Other information	1 Earth tremors frequent, several active volcanoes 2 Big tourist attraction	penguins live along the coast, but none inland, very little food, nothing to build shelter from

G Project work (Coursebook page 39)

As in the previous unit, this project has three stages. Firstly, students do some vocabulary work. In the next stage, they research and complete the table. They then use that information to complete an electronic presentation.

Coursebook materials
UNIT 5: What's an ecosystem?

Unit introduction

In this unit, the topics are **ecosystems** and **carnivorous plants**, and the Use of English areas are **word building** and **imperatives for instructions**.

A Speaking and thinking
(Coursebook pages 40–1)

1 **Pairs**

Students talk about plants, considering how we categorise or classify things. The pictures may give them some ideas.

ANSWERS: the three groups are grasses, grains, fruit-bearing plants

2 **Pairs**

Students make a copy of the table and think about who or what can eat grasses, grains and fruit-bearing plants.

ANSWERS:

Grasses	Fruit-bearing plants	Grains
cat	bear	chicken
cow	fly	human
frog	human	mouse
rabbit	mouse	
sheep	spider	
	wolf	

3 **Whole class, then pairs**

Get students to think about what animals eat, using animals that they are familiar with and they may have had contact with locally. See if they can guess the meanings of the words *herbivore* (non-meat-eating), *carnivore* (meat-eating) and *omnivore* (meat- and non-meat-eating). Point out that all three words have the same suffix (*-vore*, from the Latin verb *vorare* meaning *to devour*), and to look carefully at the three prefixes: *herbi-* (Latin for *grass* or *plant*), *carni-* (Latin for *flesh* or *meat*) and *omni-* (Latin for *all*).

4 **Alone, then pairs**

Students make a copy of the table and then add to it the animals from Activity A2. When they have completed it, get them to add two more animals to each group, if possible.

ANSWERS:

Herbivores	Carnivores	Omnivores
sheep	cat	human
cow	spider	bear
rabbit	wolf	fly
mouse		frog
chicken		

5 **Pairs**

In pairs, students talk about plants that grow in their local area and agree on a system to classify them. Then they design a classification table and add examples of plants to it. Help weaker student if necessary by suggesting plants to them.

B Reading **(Coursebook pages 41–3)**

1 **Pairs**

Students discuss what they think an *ecosystem* might be. Remind them to look at the prefix *eco-* and the suffix *-system*.

2 **Pairs**

Students match the four words with a suitable definition.

ANSWERS: interact + communicate, connect; pond + small pool of water; vast + enormous, very large; vegetation + plants

3 **Alone, then pairs**

Students skim the first paragraph of the text on page 41 and fill in gaps a–d with the four words from Activity B2.

ANSWERS: a vast, **b** vegetation, **c** pond, **d** interact

4 **Alone, then pairs**

Students now look at paragraph 2 in the text and use paper or digital reference sources to check the meaning of any unfamiliar words. They can compare the meanings they find with a partner.

5 Alone, then pairs

Moving on to paragraph 3, students fill in gaps e–h with the words in the box.

ANSWERS: e plants, **f** caterpillar, **g** birds, **h** foxes

6 Alone, then pairs

Firstly, students need to copy the ecosystem diagram into their notebooks. Then they should use the words provided to label the diagram, and compare their completed diagram with a partner's. Encourage students to talk about the ecosystem, describing what happens at each stage.

ANSWERS: a sun, **b** climate, **c/d** photosynthesis, **e** living creatures, **f/h** nutrients, **g** vegetation, **i** soil

---

DIFFERENTIATED ACTIVITY

For weaker students, provide them with some of the answers – for example c and f – so that they have fewer options to choose from. You could also provide them with a written description of the ecosystem to help them to label the diagram.

For stronger students, you could add two or three more words from the unit to the list, to act as distractors (for example *humans*, *omnivore*, *pond*). You could also provide the nine words, but with jumbled letters. Another possibility is to get your students to write a description of the ecosystem instead of simply talking about it.

C Use of English: Word building

(Coursebook page 43)

1 Whole class, then alone, then pairs

Focus on the information about word building in the green box, then get students to copy and complete the table. When they are ready, they can compare their answers with a partner.

ANSWERS:

Verb	Noun	Adjective	Adverb
split	split	split	
identify	identification/ identity	identified/ identifying	
interact	interaction	interactive	interactively
depend	dependence/ dependent	dependable	dependably

adapt	adaptation/ adapter	adaptable	
exist	existence	existing	
destroy	destruction/ destroyer	destroyed/ destroying/ destructive	destructively

D Listening (Coursebook page 44)

1 Whole class, then alone

Prepare students for the audio by checking that they understand who they are going to listen to (a teacher), what the person is going to be talking about (how to draw an ecosystem diagram) and what they have to do (follow the instructions, take notes and draw the diagram). There is quite a lot to do in this activity, so it is best to break up the listening into sections, stopping after each one and checking that students have made the necessary notes and are starting to draw the diagram. You can play the audio twice if necessary. Students can listen again in Activity D4.

TRACK 6

OK, everyone! Now that you understand the important words, such as ecosystem, climate and soil, you're ready to draw your own ecosystem diagram. Follow my instructions and write notes if you wish – you will have plenty of time to ask questions and to complete the diagram later on. When I ask you to write or draw something, I will pause to give you time.

So, first of all, imagine you're standing in a garden. What can you see and feel around you? A cat? Grass? A gentle breeze? On a piece of rough paper, make a list of as many things as you can think of. You can have about 30 seconds …

Now, choose no more than eight words from your list and write them neatly on a sheet of blank paper, leaving about 10 centimetres between them. Choose the most important words from your list – for example, sun, soil, and so on. Again, you can have about 30 seconds …

Next, choose a pair of things from your sheet which you think might be connected in some way. Draw an arrow between them and write why one needs the other – for example plants needs the sun to photosynthesise.

The next step in drawing your ecosystem diagram is to add arrows for other links between the things on your sheet. For example if water is on your sheet, this can be linked to plants, because plants need water to grow.

When you have linked things and stated why they are linked, you have nearly completed your ecosystem diagram. You may not, of course, need to link everything. Write the title *Garden ecosystem* on your sheet.

Remember that an ecosystem is a community of living things and their non-living environment. Living things are called biotic – that's b-i-o-t-i-c, and non-living things are called abiotic – that's a-b-i-o-t-i-c. A plant is biotic, whereas soil is abiotic.

On your diagram, underline in one colour everything that is biotic, and then underline everything that is abiotic in a different colour. Add a key and then your diagram is complete. How does your ecosystem diagram compare with your classmates'?

Adapted from www.pearsonpublishing.co.uk

2   Pairs
After the audio, students work with a partner and compare diagrams.

3/4 Alone, then pairs
Students read the text of the audio and put paragraphs b–g in the correct order. Make sure students understand that paragraphs a and h are in the right place already. When students are ready, play the audio again or get them to read the audioscript on pages 151–2 to check their answers.

ANSWERS: a, d, f, g, b, c, e, h

5   Alone
Students go back to the ecosystem diagram they drew in Activity D1 and check if they can make any improvements, based on the information they now have from the listening and reading activities.

E Use of English: Imperatives for instructions (Coursebook page 45)

1/2 Whole class, then alone
Go through the information in Activity E1 and check the answer to the question (b – they give you instructions). Then, in Activity E2, students should read the audioscript again and note down nine more examples of imperative verbs.

ANSWERS: there are 13 in total (students only have to choose nine): imagine, make, choose, write, choose, choose, draw, write, write, remember, underline, underline, add

3   Whole class, then pairs
Go through the instructions for Activity E3 carefully, making sure students understand what they need to do. Then get them to tell you orally what they can remember. Encourage them to use 'signpost' words and imperative verbs. Afterwards, students work with a partner to recreate the teacher's instructions for drawing an ecosystem diagram without looking back the audioscript.

DIFFERENTIATED ACTIVITY

For weaker students, you could supply the 'signpost' words and the imperative verbs. Alternatively, give students 8–10 short instructions (from the audioscript) in jumbled order and get them to reorganise the instructions. Whichever approach you use, weaker students should work with a stronger partner, but make sure that they share the work between them.

For stronger students, they can do this activity on their own, without any help.

F Writing and reading
(Coursebook pages 45–7)

1   Pairs
Students look at the picture on page 46 and answer the questions in Activity F1. Give them freedom to predict and speculate – there are no wrong answers.

2/3 Pairs
Get students to focus on the five things a carnivorous plant must be able to do above the picture (they should not read the whole text yet). Check that they understand the meaning of the words *victim*, *capture*, *attract* and *absorb*. With a partner, students put the five things into a logical order, giving reasons. Then they can read the first part of the main text to check their answers.

ANSWERS: attract, capture, kill, eat, absorb

4   Pairs
Students find words or phrases in the second section of the text that have a similar meaning to four words in Activity F4.

ANSWERS: a becomes part of the liquid = dissolves, **b** with ridges = grooved, **c** victim = prey, **d** hole = cavity

5 Pairs

For the third and final section of the text, students need to find words or phrases that have a similar meaning to the words in a–f.

ANSWERS: a bogs/swamps, **b** soil, **c** habitats, **d** soup, **e** nutrients/minerals, **f** bother

6 Whole class, then alone, then pairs

Go through the instructions carefully, checking that students understand the different stages in this writing activity. First they have to imagine that they are a hungry insect looking for food, and they need to decide which insect they are. You may need to help by supplying the English words for insects. Students also need to think about where they are, the type of food they are looking for and where to get it from. A graphic organiser like the one below may help. When students have planned everything, they write their story. Make sure they use the past tense.

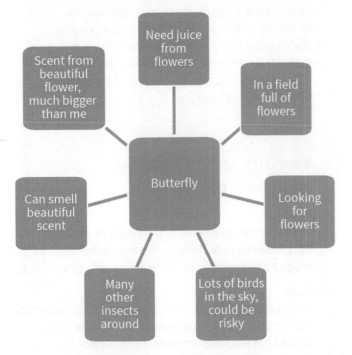

G Project work (Coursebook page 47)

1 Pairs

Students research what the six biomes are and discuss the characteristics of each one. They should consider rainfall, temperature, vegetation and the animals that live there.

2 Pairs

Now students decide where to place the six biomes on the coloured areas on the map.

ANSWERS: 1 = Polar, 2 = Temperate, 3 = Mountainous, 4 = Mediterranean, 5 = Arid, 6 = Tropical

3 Alone

For this project students need to prepare a PowerPoint presentation, using the information from the unit as well as any additional information they have gathered from Activities G1 and G2.

Coursebook materials
UNIT 6: Can bees scare elephants?

Unit introduction

In this unit, the topics are **animals** and **sea monsters**, and the Use of English areas are **infinitives and -ing forms after verbs** and **question tags**.

A Speaking and thinking
(Coursebook page 48)

1 Pairs
Students discuss what they think are the smallest and largest animals on Earth. If you think they may struggle with this, show them some pictures of small and large animals to prompt them.

2 Whole class, then pairs
Go through the information in the box, checking that students understand the abbreviations. Then students read the six statements a–f and fill in the gaps using the words from the box. There are two extra measurements and two extra animals that are not needed. See if students can give reasons for their choice of answers.

ANSWERS: a African elephant, **b** 30 metres, **c** Australian tiger beetle, **d** giant tortoise, **e** 1.5 grams, **f** bee

3/4/5 Pairs
Refer students back to Unit 5, in which they discussed the classification of plants and animals. Now, in pairs, students think about a different way for animals to be classified – for example by habitat, behaviour, how many legs they have or if they can swim or fly. Then in Activity A4 students classify the animals in the box and add more examples. Using the system given, the table would be completed as follows:

Land	Water	Land/Water
cow, bear, chicken, cat, fly, human, mouse, rabbit, sheep, spider, wolf	dolphin, shark	frog

B Reading (Coursebook pages 49–50)

1/2 Pairs
Students discuss the three questions. There are no right or wrong answers, so allow students to talk freely. Get feedback from the whole class so that students can compare their ideas.

3 Pairs
Students work together and check the meaning of the words and phrases in the box, using paper or digital reference sources for help.

4 Pairs
Check that students understand the meaning of *sting*. Working in pairs, they then decide if the information a–g is true or false. They will find out if they are right or wrong when they read the text, so do not provide any feedback yet.

5/6 Alone, then pairs
Students work alone to read the text on page 50 to check their answers to Activities B3 and B4. Then they can compare answers with a partner.

ANSWERS: e and g are false; the rest are true

7 Alone
Students read the seven things that Lucy did and put them into the correct order. Then they re-read paragraphs 4 and 5 to check.

ANSWERS: paragraph 2, 6, 7, 1, 4, 3, 5

C Use of English: Infinitives and -ing forms after verbs
(Coursebook pages 50-1)

1 Whole class, then pairs
Go through the information about infinitives and -ing forms after verbs in the blue box, then get students to do Activity C1. They need to decide which verbs in the box are followed by an infinitive verb, and which by an -ing form. They also need to consider if any can be followed by to + -ing. Do the first one as an example.

ANSWERS:

	to + infinitive	-ing	to + -ing
admit		✓	✓
afford	✓		
agree	✓		
arrange	✓		
ask	✓		
avoid		✓	
decide	✓		
deny		✓	
enjoy		✓	
fail	✓		
learn	✓		
manage	✓		
miss		✓	
need	✓		
promise	✓		
recommend		✓	
refuse	✓		
suggest		✓	
want	✓		

2 Pairs
Point out that some verbs can be followed by either to + infinitive or -ing, and that sometimes there is no difference in meaning while at other times there is a difference in meaning. Students look at the two sentences and decide if the use of to + infinitive or -ing makes any difference to the meaning (it doesn't).

3 Pairs
With other verbs, the meaning does change. Here, students should decide what the difference in meaning is.
ANSWER: a = took a break from one activity to do another activity (buy some chocolate), b = took a break from doing something on a regular basis (buying chocolate)

4 Pairs
Students look at the pairs of sentences and decide if there is any difference in meaning and, if so, what it is.

ANSWERS:
a i try to do = attempt, ii try doing = test something to see if it works or not or to see if you like it
b i regret doing = feel sorry about a situation, perhaps something that you wish you hadn't done, ii regret to do = to say that you feel sorry about having to do something
c i remember to do = not to forget to do something, ii remember doing = remember something from the past, keep it in your mind

5 Pairs
This activity gives students the chance to practise the verb forms covered in this section. First, each student writes down seven questions to ask their partner, using the verbs enjoy, hate, forget, recommend and regret, plus two verbs of their own choice. Then the pairs take it in turns to ask/answer the questions. Monitor the activity carefully and make sure students are using the correct forms.

D Listening (Coursebook page 52)

1 Whole class
Ask the class if they know the word for a creature with no backbone (invertebrate) and if they can name any.

2 Pairs
Students look at the list of creatures in the box and check if they thought of any in the previous activity. They should then choose which ones are invertebrates (they all are).

3 Pairs
Give students enough time to work through the list and decide if the information is true or false, using paper or digital reference sources to check anything they do not understand. If time is an issue, you could allocate different pieces of information to different students and then gather class feedback. Do not tell students if they are right or wrong, as they will find out for themselves in the following activities.

4 Alone, then pairs
Prepare students for the audio, checking that they understand who and what they are going to listen to, and what they have to do. When students are ready, they listen and number the creatures from Activity D2 in the order that they hear them. Afterwards, they should check their answers with a partner.

TRACK 7

Caterina Russo: In today's 'Science Weekly' programme, we are going to be talking with Dr Ahmed Al Ajmee about invertebrates, some of the world's most amazing animals! Welcome, Dr Al Ajmee.

Dr Ajmee: Thank you, Caterina.

Caterina: These invertebrates are special, aren't they, Doctor?

Dr A: Yes, very special. They often appear alien to us and so we fear them. For example, jellyfish have no eyes, and worms have no recognisable head, but some invertebrates are highly intelligent.

CR: Really? You're not serious, are you?

Dr A: Well, octopuses can unscrew jar lids to get at food and they can quickly learn skills by observing others. Another example is the robber crab, which can climb palm trees to cut down coconuts.

CR: That's amazing! But what about insects? I think they are very common, aren't they?

Dr A: Yes, they are. Insects are the most common animals on Earth, with over 1 million species, including butterflies, beetles, flies, wasps and grasshoppers. Some scientists believe that there may still be 10 million species of insect that we have yet to discover.

CR: And the insects show some similarities to humans, don't they?

Dr A: In some ways, yes. Insects do not have an internal skeleton like we do, but, instead, they have a hard exterior. However, they find food together and fight off enemies, just as we do!

CR: And it's true, isn't it, that millions of ants may live together in one nest?

Dr A: Yes, they are called 'workers', and their job is simply to serve their queen. Her only job is to lay eggs.

CR: What about spiders? They have to be the most frightening insects, don't they?

Dr A: Well, spiders and scorpions are not insects. They are classified as arachnids, and, as you say, they are considered very frightening for some people.

CR: But that fear is justified, isn't it?

Dr A: In some cases, yes. One species of Mexican scorpion kills more than one thousand people every year, and it is claimed that the poison from the black widow spider is 15 times more powerful than a rattlesnake's.

CR: Giant squid were once thought to be sea monsters, weren't they?

Dr A: Well, in 1887, the body of a giant squid was washed up on the beach in New Zealand. It measured 18.9 metres from the tip of its tail to the end of its tentacles, so it's no surprise people thought it was a monster! Since then, more bodies have been found, but very few people have ever seen a living giant squid. The world's largest invertebrates remain a great mystery to modern science.

CR: Dr Ahmed, one final question: what is the most dangerous invertebrate to humans? It has to be something that lives in the sea, doesn't it?

Dr A: No, not at all! It's the mosquito. It spreads diseases, such as malaria, which kill thousands of people every year.

CR: I would never have guessed! Thank you again for telling us so much, and you will come back again soon, won't you?

Adapted from *The Kingfisher Facts and Records Book* (Kingfisher Publications, 2000).

ANSWERS: 1 jellyfish, **2** worm, **3** octopus, **4** crab, **5** butterfly, **6** beetle, **7** grasshopper, **8** ant, **9** spider, **10** scorpion, **11** squid, **12** mosquito

5 **Alone**
Students listen again to check if the information in Activity D3 is true or false. They should correct anything that is false, then compare their answers with a partner.

ANSWERS:
True: b, e, f, g, h
False: a (jellyfish have no eyes), c (1 million), d (only in some ways), i (only a few people), j (mosquito)

6 **Pairs**
Students work together to find the answers to questions a–f. See how much they can remember before referring them to the audioscript on page 152.

ANSWERS:
a octopus – can unscrew jar lids to get food and (robber) crab – can climb palm trees to get coconuts
b find food together, fight off enemies, live together
c to lay eggs
d a spider is not an insect (arachnid)
e it's 15 times more powerful
f enthusiastic – he's very knowledgeable and easily understood

E Use of English: Question tags
(Coursebook page 53)

1/2 Whole class, then pairs

Focus on the information about question tags in the green box, then get students to re-read the audioscript from the previous section and identify eight more question tags. They need to write them in a list in their notebooks. For each one, they should decide whether the interviewer's voice goes up or down, and mark it accordingly (as in the Coursebook examples).

ANSWERS: aren't they (down), don't they (up), isn't it (down), don't they (down), isn't it (up), weren't they (up), doesn't it (up), won't you (down)

3 Alone

Students copy and complete the rules a–d, basing their answers on the examples in Activity E2.

ANSWERS: a negative, **b** negative, **c** (question) tag, **d** *do*

4 Alone, then pairs

Students work alone to add question tags to the statements a–i, and then check them with a partner by reading them aloud, with the correct intonation.

ANSWERS:

a aren't they?
b aren't there?
c aren't they?
d hasn't it?
e doesn't it/she?
f are they?
g isn't it?
h have they?
i doesn't it?

F Reading and writing
(Coursebook pages 54–5)

1/2 Whole class, then alone

Check if students have heard of the story *Twenty Thousand Leagues Under the Sea* and, if so, what they know about it. You could show them a book or DVD cover, or even a short clip from the film adaptation of the book. Then students skim the text to get a general idea of the story. If you prefer, you could read it aloud to them.

3 Pairs

Students read the text more carefully and focus on the words and phrases printed in red, working with their partner to make sure they understand the

meanings. They can use paper or digital reference sources for help. When they are ready, get students to give you an oral summary of the text.

4/5 Alone

Students are going to read a translation (from French into English) of the end of the story. There is some quite challenging vocabulary here, so deal with this first, but do not burden students with too many words that won't be useful once they have understood the text (e.g. *maelstrom, heartily*). The purpose is to prepare students for some creative writing, in which they take on the role of one of the main characters and describe what happened that night. Encourage students to respond to the questions the narrator asks in the final two paragraphs of the story (these are repeated in Activity F5 in the Coursebook).

DIFFERENTIATED ACTIVITY

For weaker students, advise them not to worry about taking on the role of one of the main characters, but instead to imagine that they themselves were on board the *Nautilus*. You could also simplify the question prompts and reduce the number of questions.

For stronger students, encourage them to be as creative as possible. You could increase the challenge level by asking them to write a dialogue between two of the main characters, imagining that both were present that night. A follow-up activity could be to report what the two characters said to each other.

G Project work (Coursebook page 55)

1/2 Alone

For this project, students are going to produce a graph or chart about different types and sizes of invertebrates, including information that they find out themselves. They can choose how to present their findings – either a poster, leaflet or PowerPoint presentation.

Coursebook materials
UNIT 7: Can penguins see under water?

Unit introduction

In this unit, the topics are **human and animal senses** and **chess**, and the Use of English areas are **comparative adverbs** and **-ing forms as subjects and after prepositions**.

A Speaking and thinking
(Coursebook pages 56–7)

1   Pairs
Students discuss how our five senses provide us with information about the outside world, for example by 'feeling' the temperature, by our eyes reacting to different levels of light and our ears hearing different types of sound. Each picture depicts one sense.
ANSWERS: 1 = smell (nose), 2 = sight (eyes), 3 = taste (tongue), 4 = hearing (ears), 5 = touch (fingers, etc.)

2   Pairs, then whole class
Students work together to answer questions a–f. This should be a free discussion, as for the most part there are no right or wrong answers. Monitor students, but do not interfere unless help is required. Allow some time for class feedback, so that students can share their ideas.

3   Whole class, then pairs
Go through the information A–J with students, dealing with any vocabulary issues. Then get them to work in pairs to decide if the information is true or false. Students will find out in the next section, so there is no need to supply answers at this point.

B Listening (Coursebook pages 57–8)

1/2 Whole class, then pairs
Prepare students for the audio by checking that they understand who and what they are going to listen to, and what they have to do. Firstly, they need to look at the words in the box and complete the activities a–c. They should also add three more words to each group if they can.

ANSWERS:

1 Sight	2 Touch	3 Taste	4 Hearing
air	feel	buds	frequencies
eyeball	pressure	sense	hearing
eyes	sense	taste	Hz
lens	touch	tongue	sense
movement			sound
sense			
vision			

3   Alone, then pairs
Students listen to the audio and check if the information in Activity A3 is true or false (it is all true), and compare their answers with a partner.

TRACK 8

Abdullah al Wahaibi: Welcome to today's show. I'm going to be talking to two IGCSE students from the Emirates High School about animals and their senses. My guests today are Moosa and Hessa, and they have a list of questions ready to ask me. Welcome to both of you.

Moosa al Issa & Hessa al Nader: Hello, Abdullah.

HN: Abdullah, our first question is about sight. Do animals and humans have the same sight abilities?

AW: Not at all. Sight is a very important sense and many animals have incredible powers of vision. Humans have two eyes with a lens in each, but some animals have many more. Did you know that a dragonfly has 30,000 lenses in each eye, and even that fly that's buzzing around your food has 3000? This allows them to see a lot better than humans can.

MI: Wow, I never knew that! Abdullah, why can't we see clearly under water?

AW: Hmm … it's very annoying when you go swimming and you can't see clearly under water without a mask, isn't it? Well, penguins have a type of eye mask that allows them to see more clearly than humans. Consequently, they are also able to move faster through the water. And see that eagle flying way up high? Well, its eyeballs are bigger than yours! An eagle's eyeball length is about 35 millimetres.

HN: So how big is my eyeball?

AW: Yours is only 24 millimetres.

MI: I've heard that some animals can cross their eyes – is that true, Abdullah?

AW: Yes, it's true. Weird, isn't it? Chameleons can move their eyes independently and so they can look in two different directions at the same time.

MI: Isn't that cool!

AW: And some animals have adapted their sight so much that they have multiple eyes.

HN: You're kidding us, right?

AW: Not in the least! A scorpion can have up to 12 eyes and the scary box jellyfish has double that number. And did you know that some spiders have eight eyes?

MI: Imagine if they moved independently, like the chameleon's! Scary!

HN: What about touch, Abdullah? Tell us something about how animals feel things.

AW: Insects often have a wonderful sense of touch and ants can feel movement through 5 centimetres of earth. Also, a snake knows when a mouse is 40 centimetres away simply by sensing its body temperature.

MI: Someone told me that flies use their feet to smell. That can't be true!

AW: Well, the truth is that flies use the hairs on their feet not to feel, but to taste, and those butterflies in your garden are using hairs on their wings to detect changes in air pressure.

HN: Animals are really cool, aren't they? What about hearing? Bats hear far better than humans, don't they?

AW: Yes, and, in fact, they can hear much better than any other living creature. Humans can hear sound frequencies between 20 and 20,000 hertz, and mice can hear much better – between 1000 and 100,000 hertz. But bats can detect sound up to 120,000 hertz. Maybe that's why they have bigger ears than you?!

HN & MI: [laughter]

MI: OK, last sense – taste. What can you tell us, Abdullah?

AW: OK! Which animal do you think has the best ability to taste: a human, a rabbit, a catfish or a snake? Moosa?

MI: No idea! Maybe the rabbit? What do you think, Hessa?

HN: Ummm … a snake?

AW: Both wrong! You have about 10,000 taste buds on your tongue, a rabbit has 17,000, while a catfish has up to 100,000! Our poor old friend, the snake, has none – it uses its tongue to smell and sends this information to the brain. Crazy snake! Now, which animal would you prefer to be?! Thanks to Moosa and Hessa … see you all next week!

4   Alone, then pairs
For the second listening, students are going to focus on the numbers mentioned during the interview. First they should make a copy of the table, then they should listen again and make a written note about each number. Afterwards, they can check their answers with a partner and refer to the audioscript if necessary.

ANSWERS:
35 mm = eagle's eyeball length
40 cm = distance from which a snake can sense a mouse
20 = lower level of sound frequency (hertz) for human hearing
120,000 = upper level of sound frequency for bats
17,000 = number of taste buds on rabbit's tongue
0 = number of taste buds on snake's tongue

5   Pairs
Numbers in English can be quite difficult to say correctly, so this activity gives students an opportunity to practise some. They have already heard all the numbers in the audio, but you may wish to model them again.

C Use of English: Comparative adverbs (Coursebook pages 58–9)

1   Whole class, then pairs
Focus on the information about comparative adverbs in the green box, and then get students to look at Activity C1. They need to make complete sentences that include a verb and a comparative adverb. Do the first question as an example, then students can work together to make the other sentences.

28

ANSWERS:

a A black mamba snake moves a little more slowly than an elephant.

b A cheetah can run considerably faster than a mouse.

c A blue whale swims far more beautifully than a bottlenose whale.

d Sufian arrives slightly earlier for school than Fathi.

e Naziha studied much harder than Sally.

2 Alone

Students now practise using comparative adverbs in sentences of their own. They can use the verbs and adverbs in the box or their own words if they prefer.

D Reading (Coursebook pages 59–61)

1 Whole class

All the words mean *chess*. If the students' own language is not represented in the box, get them to tell you how to say *chess* in their language.

2/3/4 Pairs, then whole class

Students work together and answer the questions in these three activities. Open up the discussion to the whole class so that students can hear one another's ideas.

5 Alone

Students focus on the first part of the text (sections i–iv) and check if their ideas in Activity D4 were correct (what assistance is given to visually impaired chess players).

6 Pairs

Students work together to check the meaning of the six words, using paper or digital reference sources if necessary. They should then skim the whole text and fill in the gaps using the six words.

ANSWERS: a modifications, b determine, c projection, d securely, e distinguish, f opponent

7 Alone, then pairs

Students work alone to answer the questions, then check with their partner. Remind them to look for key word/s in the questions, and to think about the type of answer each question requires.

ANSWERS:

a the black squares are a different height from the white squares

b so that pieces can be fixed

c each piece has a nail in its base

d black pieces have a pin fixed to the head

e by using three things: feeling the raised squares, feeling the shape, by touching the pin

f writes it in Braille and audio records

E Use of English: *-ing* forms as subjects and after prepositions (Coursebook pages 61–3)

1 Whole class

Focus on the information about *-ing* forms as subjects and after prepositions in the green box, then get students to look back at the text and find more examples of *-ing* forms.

ANSWERS: *by feeling*, *by touching*, *after making*

2 Alone, then pairs

The next article, some of which is in note form, is about a young musician who plays the piano using only his left hand. Students should complete activities a–d on their own, then check their answers with a partner.

ANSWERS:

a Although he was sometimes disappointed, McCarthy says that he learned to be positive and to welcome the challenges that come with <u>playing</u> with one hand.

c After <u>graduating</u> he said it was a fantastic experience.

d It was quite emotional. Four years of <u>working</u> with a lot of different people.

e After <u>releasing</u> his own album, he received the International AMI award for creative excellence in music.

f According to McCarthy, <u>playing</u> pieces just for the left hand made <u>practising</u> more interesting.

g <u>Playing</u> at Carnegie Hall in New York and <u>making</u> a record deal are two of McCarthy's dreams.

3 Alone, then pairs

Students read the text again and answer questions a–f, then compare their answers with a partner.

ANSWERS:

a because he loved the piano so much

b positive/determined/focused/strong

c to impress audiences

d makes practising more interesting

e the piano pedals

f yes, by believing in yourself

F Writing (Coursebook page 63)

1   Whole class, then alone
Focus on the instructions for this writing activity, checking that students understand who the audience is (school magazine readers), and that they are writing from the personal experience of attending one of Nicholas McCarthy's concerts. They can use information from the unit as well as their own ideas. They should use the bullet points as prompts to guide their writing.

G Project work (Coursebook page 63)

For this project, students need to research three different games of their choice, then copy and complete the table in the Coursebook, using the example to guide them. Then they choose one of their three games and design a classroom noticeboard poster, which should include pictures and other visuals.

Coursebook materials
UNIT 8: How hot are chilli peppers?

Unit introduction

In this unit, the topics are **chilli peppers**, **healthy food** and **being a healthy teen**, and the Use of English areas are **referring words** and **quantifiers**.

A Speaking and thinking
(Coursebook page 64)

1 Pairs
Remind students of some of the meanings of *hot* that were discussed in Unit 4, one of which was *spicy*. Get them to think about other foods that could be described as *spicy*. They should then discuss in pairs if they have a favourite spicy food and talk about who cooks food for them.

2 Pairs
Students talk about some of the natural ingredients that we can add to food to improve its flavour, such as onions, and make a list.

3/4 Pairs
Here are six ingredients (as anagrams) that are often added to food to improve (or at least change) its flavour. Students unscramble the letters and then discuss which ones they think are healthy, which are not and which ones can make food spicy hot.

ANSWERS: **a** onion, **b** chilli, **c** garlic, **d** pepper, **e** salt, **f** sugar
a, b, c & d can all make food taste spicier, but taste is a very personal thing

B Reading (Coursebook pages 64–5)

1 Alone, then pairs
Students work on their own and decide if statements a–g are true or false. They can then discuss this with a partner. You can either allow them to use paper or digital reference sources to look up any challenging words or phrases (for example *soothe a sore throat*, *scientific scale*), or deal with them yourself. Do not tell the students yet if the information is true or false, as they will find out for themselves when they read the text.

2 Pairs
You could give students a handout with the four headings in separate columns for them to complete. They need to add the other pieces of information from Activity B1, then predict anything else they might read in the text.

ANSWERS:

A chilli history	Chilli heat	Grow your own	Chilli health
more than 400 types	*Scoville scale measures heat in chillies*	*can be grown indoors*	*full of vitamin A* *can help soothe a sore throat* *can take away headaches* *improve digestion*

3 Alone
Students skim the text and check if the information from Activity B1 is true or false (it is all true).

4 Groups of four, then whole class
Divide the class into A/B/C/D groups. Then split them into groups of the same letter. A students look at words and phrases a–e, B students at f–j, C students at k–o, and D students at p–t. Each group finds words or phrases in the text that have a similar meaning to the words and phrases allocated to them. When each group has finished, students should form A/B/C/D groups and share their answers so that each new group has the answers to all the questions.

ANSWERS:
a mild
b indigenous
c cultivated
d rate
e potent
f triggers
g relieve
h minimal
i indoors
j edible

k loaded
l boosts
m immune
n mature
o gradually
p thermal
q calories
r sweat
s evaporates
t sore

5 **Alone, then pairs**
Quickly go through the questions a–h, dealing with any difficult vocabulary, and getting students to underline the key words, and think about the types of answers required. Then students write their answers before checking with their partner.

ANSWERS:
a 10 (counting Central and South America as two)
b tasting
c capsaicin
d it triggers the brain to produce painkillers (endorphins)
e 80% (8 out of 10)
f minimum growth area, warm climate, under glass, grow well in pots, can be grown indoors
g because of high levels of capsaicin, which speeds up body's metabolic rate
h full of vitamin A, antioxidant, vitamin C, improves digestion (thermal effect), burns off calories, helps to removes aches and pains and helps sore throats

6 **Pairs**
First clearly model all the phrases with numbers from the text. Then students can practise saying the phrases to each other.

C Use of English: Referring words (Coursebook pages 67–8)

1 **Whole class, then pairs**
Go through the information about referring words in the blue box, then get students to look again at the text and find some more examples of referring words, saying which word or phrase is being referred to (Activity C1).

ANSWERS:
this refers back to *measuring the strength of capsicums*
which refers back to *computers*
they refers back to *Chillies*
They refers back to *Chillies*

their refers back to *capsaicin levels*
these refers back to *capsaicin levels … at their highest*

2 **Pairs, then alone**
Students skim read the second text (on page 68) and fill in the gaps a–k in paragraphs 1–3 with the words from the box. Then they can check with a partner.

ANSWERS:
a these (the comments mentioned in the text)
b they (your parents)
c their (your parents)
d they (your parents)
e your (the reader)
f your (the reader)
g it (your breakfast)
h you (teens)
i this (breakfast)
j any (food in packets etc.)
k it (the packet etc.)

3 **Pairs**
In paragraphs 4 and 5, there are 14 more gaps. Working with a partner, students should fill in each gap with a suitable referring word, and decide what the word is referring back to.

ANSWERS:
l it (exercise)
m your (the reader)
n it (dancing)
o This (dancing/exercise)
p you (the reader)
q it (physical activity)
r your (the reader)
s It (physical activity)
t your (the reader)
u your (the reader)
v it/this (physical activity)
w your (the reader's)
x your (the reader's)
y it (your body)

D Listening (Coursebook pages 68–9)

1 **Whole class, then pairs**
Prepare students for the audio, asking them who and what they are going to be listening to (someone talking about how rainforest plants are used in food products and medicines). Before they listen, students talk together about what plants grow in a rainforest (such as rubber) and make a list. If you think students may struggle with this, you could show them some pictures of rainforest

2 **Alone**

Students listen to the audio and check if any of the plants from their list in Activity D1 are mentioned. They should also note the name of one animal.

TRACK 9

[1] Even though hundreds of rainforest plants are used in modern medicines and as food products, less than 1% of all of them have been checked for use on humans. Only a few hundred of around 3 million species have been investigated.

[2] It is estimated that 25% of all our medicines come from plants growing in the rainforest. For example, Vincristine, a drug taken from a plant in Madagascar, has allowed an 80% improvement for some forms of children's cancer.

[3] Curare, a poison used by Amazonian Indians on arrows, can be used to relax muscles, helping people who suffer from various diseases. More than 2000 tropical rainforest plants with the potential to fight cancer have been identified. Yet, as the forests are destroyed, such plants are lost forever. Animals, too, can provide medicine. The armadillo is being used to help find a cure for leprosy.

[4] Many of our familiar food crops, such as maize and banana, originated from wild rainforest plants. Many food sources are still being discovered in rainforests. The peach palm of Brazil produces up to 300 peach-like fruits a year. The fruit has twice the food value of a banana, and more protein and carbohydrate than maize. Who knows how many more valuable foods are waiting to be discovered.

[5] Spices, palm oils, rubber – every day we use products from the rainforest. As the trees are destroyed, so too is a great amount of knowledge. The indigenous rainforest tribes, whose lives are also disrupted as forests are cleared, know far more than we do about the plants and animals around them. In north-western Amazonia alone, the Indians use over 1300 plant species as medicines. The native tribes have lived in the rainforests for thousands of years without causing them any long-term damage. We have a lot to learn from them.

adapted from www.ypte.org.uk

ANSWER: *armadillo* is mentioned in the third paragraph

3 **Alone, then pairs**

Students listen a second time and order the figures as they hear them.

ANSWERS: 1%, 3 million, 25%, 80%, 2000, 300, 1300

4 **Pairs**

Students read the sentences and fill in the gaps using the figures from Activity D3. They can check by looking at the audioscript on page 153.

ANSWERS: a 1%, b 1300, c 300, d 3 million, e 2000, f 80%, g 25%

5 **Pairs**

This activity gives students more practice in saying numbers. Give students a clear model for each sentence, after which they should practise saying the sentences to each other.

6 **Alone**

Allow students time to write their own paragraph about how rainforest plants are used, using the information they have learnt in this section.

E Use of English: Quantifiers
(Coursebook pages 69–70)

1 **Whole class, then pairs**

Go through the information about quantifiers in the blue box, then get students to work together to add more single-word and multi-word quantifiers to a copy of the table.

POSSIBLE ANSWERS:

Single-word quantifiers	Multi-word quantifiers
any, few, some, a, an, much, many, few, half, three, either, your, such, little, no, etc.	hundreds (thousands, millions, 100s, 25%) of, plenty of, one of the, a variety of, a bit (lack, great deal) of, less than 1% of, only a few, more than, many of, a great (small) amount of, over 1300, etc.

2 **Alone, then pairs**

Students read the audioscript on page 153 and see how many more quantifiers they can find. Remind them that quantifiers are followed by a noun or a noun phrase.

3 **Alone, then pairs**

Students practise using quantifiers by completing the gaps in the sentences a–i.

POSSIBLE ANSWERS: a some, b many, c Many, d many, e hundreds of, f a variety of, g a few, h plenty of, i some of, none

F Writing (Coursebook pages 70–1)

1 Whole class, then pairs

Make sure that students understand what they are going to read about (school canteens in Delhi) and then focus on the four pieces of information a–d, **before students look at the text**. Get them to predict what they might find out about the information. You could use A/B/ C/D groups, allocating one piece of information to each group to discuss, and then share with the whole class. Afterwards, students read the text and check their predictions.

ANSWERS:

a for health reasons
b some have banned junk food on school premises
c stop street sellers and shops near schools selling junk food
d old – crisps, biscuits, chocolate, fizzy drinks
new – protein-based food, fresh fruit juices

2 Alone, then pairs

Students write a letter to their headteacher explaining why the school canteen needs to improve its menu and suggest who the school can get help from. Students can use the information given in this unit, as well their own ideas, in their writing.

G Project work (Coursebook page 71)

For this project, students design an information leaflet about a rainforest plant for the class noticeboard. They need to research two of the products discussed in the unit (maize, banana, spices, palm oils, rubber), using a copy of the table for their notes, and then select one to focus on in their information leaflet.

Coursebook materials
UNIT 9: Who was Ibn Battuta?

Unit introduction

In this unit, the topics are **travellers and explorers** and **NASA**, and the Use of English areas are **countries, nationalities and languages** and **past perfect**.

A Speaking and thinking
(Coursebook page 73)

1   Whole class, then pairs
Introduce the topic of explorers and exploring, and get students to think about what exactly explorers did (and do). Focus on the words *explored*, *discovered*, *navigated*, *guided*, *interpreted*, *negotiated*, *sailed*, *climbed*, and get students to use paper or digital reference sources to check the meaning of each one.

2/3 Pairs
Students talk together and answer questions a–d. If they struggle with the names and giving information about any explorers, you could immediately move on to Activity A3 and have some extra information about each explorer ready.
ANSWERS: 1 = Ibn Battuta, 2 = Jacques Cousteau, 3 = Eric the Red, 4 = Abel Tasman, 5 = Mae C. Jemison, 6 = Tenzing Norgay, 7 = Chang Ch'ien, 8 = Christopher Columbus

4   Alone, then pairs
Students skim the information on the following page and then work with their partner to answer questions a–c.
ANSWERS:
a *c.* = 'circa' (about), BCE = 'before common era' (before modern times)
b we are not sure about the exact date
c h (Mae C. Jemison)

5   Pairs
Students work together to complete the timeline, using the information from the text. They should make a copy of the timeline in their notebooks, then match the travellers in Activity A3 with the information a–h, and write the names in the correct time box.
ANSWERS:
a Chang Ch'ien
b Eric the Red
c Ibn Battuta
d Christopher Columbus
e Abel Tasman
f Jacques Cousteau
g Tenzing Norgay
h Mae C. Jemison

6   Pairs, then whole class
Students work together to discuss whether or not they admire any of the travellers, and give their reasons. They should also mention any further information they know about the travellers.

7   Alone
If students have access to a classroom map or one from the Internet, they should use it to find all the places mentioned in the text in Activity A5.

B Reading **(Coursebook pages 74–6)**

1   Pairs
Students already know a few things about Ibn Battuta from the previous section. Now they are going to add to this knowledge by discussing the questions a–e, using paper or digital reference sources for help. You do not need to correct any information they find, as they can do this for themselves when the read the next text.
ANSWERS: a Tangier, **b** to make the pilgrimage to Mecca, **c** nearly 30, **d** China, **e** because of his writing

2   Pairs
Students work together to check the meaning of the words and phrases given, all of which appear in the text about Ibn Battuta. They can use paper or digital reference sources for help, but tell them not to look at the text itself. You could put the words on the board or on a handout and get students to do the activity with their books closed. Whichever approach you choose, make sure everyone understands all the words and phrases.

DIFFERENTIATED ACTIVITY

For weaker students – or if time is an issue – share the words and phrases among groups (a–d, e–i and j–m) so that students have less to work on. You could also provide definitions for some of the words and phrases so students can match them.

For stronger students, once they have checked the meanings, you could ask them to use some of the words and phrases in sentences of their own.

3 Alone
Students read the text about Ibn Battuta and check their understanding of the words and phrases in orange (the ones from Activity B2).

DIFFERENTIATED ACTIVITY

For weaker students, allocate each (or a couple) of the five paragraphs to different students, so that their reading load is decreased.

For stronger students, you could supply them with a copy of the text with all the orange words and phrases removed. Students then have to fill in the gaps using the words and phrases from Activity B2.

4 Pairs
Refer students back to Activity B1 and their ideas about the five questions a–e. Get them to compare their ideas with the information in the text, adding or changing anything if necessary.

5 Alone, then pairs
For the final activity in this section, students make a copy of the table and then work on their own to fill in as many gaps as possible. Remind them that they won't be able to write something in every gap. They can compare their table with a partner afterwards.

ANSWERS:

C Use of English: Countries, nationalities and languages
(Coursebook page 76)

1 Whole class, then pairs
Go through the information about countries, nationalities and languages in the blue box, then get students to look again at the information in Activity A4 and make a list of all the countries and nationalities that are mentioned. Using a classroom map or one from the Internet, they should then find all the places on their list.

ANSWERS: Chinese, Uzbekistan, China, Norwegian, Iceland, Viking, European, Greenland, Morocco, Africa, Middle East, Levant, Russia, Italian, America, Europe, Netherlands, East Indies, New Zealand, Tonga Islands, Fiji, France, Nepal, American, Morocco, Egypt, Swahili, Anatolia, Persia, Afghanistan, India, Sri Lanka, Maldives

2/3 Pairs
Students make a copy of the table in their notebooks, add the words from their list in Activity C1, then complete all the other columns. They should also add their own country, if it is not already listed. For Activity C3, students need to find out about Poland, Turkey, Wales, Cyprus, Swaziland and Indonesia, and add information about these countries to the table.

D Reading and writing
(Coursebook pages 77–8)

1/2 Pairs, then whole class
Students think about the type of equipment that the travellers mentioned in the unit used to help them. They should consider what equipment travellers from a thousand years ago had access to compared with modern-day explorers. Their list might include Christopher Columbus – compass, Mae C. Jemison – sophisticated communications

Verb	Noun (person)	Noun (thing)	Adjective	Adverb
shorten			short	shortly
travel	traveller	travel	travelled, travelling	
		curiosity	curious	curiously
complete		completion	complete	completely
		tradition	traditional	traditionally
possess	possessor	possession	possessive	possessively
observe	observer	observation	observant	observantly

equipment, etc. For Activity D2, pairs should consider questions a–c and be prepared to give reasons for their answers to the class

3 Pairs
Make sure students understand the word *oceanographer*, then get them to talk about the questions.

4 Pairs
Students work together to match the words and phrases in column A with a suitable definition from column B.

ANSWERS:
interactions = ways of communicating
unique = special, different from others
remote = far away
crew = staff on ship
consistent = reliable
a mixed blessing = having advantages and disadvantages
respondents = those who answer questions
primary appeals = important attractions
onshore = on land
fulfil = achieve or satisfy
substitute = replace

5 Alone
Now students skim the text on page 78 and check which (if any) of the forms of communication from Activity D3 are available to oceanographer Cassandra Lopez (they are all mentioned in the reading text).

6/7 Pairs
First students read the text again and find all the words and phrases from Activity D4, checking that they fully understand the meanings. They should then copy and complete the table with the advantages and disadvantages of advanced on-board communications systems.

ANSWERS:

Advantages	Disadvantages
People can be alone, but have chance to tell others	You can never get away from modern life
Ship can operate better	Communications interrupt personal life
Researchers and crew can maintain relationships with family and friends	Crew worry about home
	Communications often inconsistent

8 Alone, then pairs
Students work alone to answer questions a–g. Remind them to find the key word/s and to think about the type of answer required for each question. Then students compare their answers with a partner.

ANSWERS:
a she was on location in the Southern Ocean
b people who want to get away from it all, but still blog
c scientific research and maintaining contact with home
d to tell people about their experiences
e he uses a real-time camera system
f both
g interruptions and difficulties with real relationships

E Use of English: Past perfect
(Coursebook page 79)

1 Whole class, then alone, then pairs
Go through the information about the past perfect tense in the blue box and the example in Activity E1, then get students to join the sentences together.

POSSIBLE ANSWERS:
a Christopher Columbus arrived in America 500 years after the Vikings had landed there.
b Jacques Cousteau had studied marine life before he became a film maker and scientist.
c By the time Chang Ch'ien introduced grapes in China he had travelled west to Samarkand and Uzbekistan.
d Tenzing Norgay died in 1986, 33 years after he had reached the summit of Everest in 1953 with Edmund Hillary.

F Listening and writing
(Coursebook pages 79–80)

1 Pairs
Students talk about the specific skills they think travellers or adventurers need, and if they need any specific training before they start their journey. Students should also consider whether or not there are any job advertisements for travellers and adventurers!

2 Pairs
Find out what students already know about NASA, then in pairs get them to discuss the three prompt questions.

37

3 Whole class, then pairs

Prepare students for the audio by making sure they understand what they are going to listen to. Before they listen, they should look at the eight phrases a–h on page 80, and use paper or digital reference sources to check the meanings of any words or phrases they are unfamiliar with.

4 Alone, then pairs

Now students listen to the audio and number the words and phrases from Activity F3 in the order that they hear them.

TRACK 10

Welcome to 'Science Tomorrow'. Our first item today comes from the USA, where NASA, which is the National Aeronautics and Space Administration, has just announced an Exploration Design Challenge. This amazing event is designed to give students, from kindergarten through to grade 12, the opportunity to play a unique role in the future of human spaceflight.

The challenge asks students to think and act like scientists to overcome one of the major hurdles for deep-space long-duration exploration: protecting astronauts and hardware from the dangers of deep-space radiation. The goal is to help students see their role in the future of exploration endeavours, which will require new technologies and ambitious minds.

We know that space exploration has inspired and fascinated young people for generations, and NASA's Exploration Design Challenge is a unique way to capture and engage the imaginations of tomorrow's engineers and scientists. That's you, listeners!

NASA and its partners are developing the Orion spacecraft to carry astronauts farther into space than humans ever have gone before. To do this, materials must be engineered for the spacecraft that will better protect future space explorers from the dangers of space radiation. Before the end of the decade, NASA's Space Launch System heavy-lift rocket, currently in development, will send Orion on a flight-test mission around the moon.

The Challenge brings cutting-edge learning to educators and students using various activities, as well as print and video resources developed by leading education experts. Students taking part in the challenge will discover how to plan and design improved radiation shielding aboard the new spacecraft.

Younger students, in grades KG–4 and 5–8, will analyse different materials that simulate space radiation shielding for Orion and recommend materials that block harmful radiation and protect astronauts. Students in grades 9–12 will learn about radiation and human space travel in greater detail. Using what they have learned, they will be asked to think and act like engineers by designing shielding that protects a sensor on the Orion capsule from space radiation.

If you want to learn more about the Exploration Design Challenge and sign up to become a virtual crew member, visit: http://www.nasa.gov/education/edc. If NASA's education programmes interest you, visit: http://www.nasa.gov/education. And if you didn't have time to write down the web pages, you can find them on our own site, www.sciencetomorrow.eur.

Adapted from www.nasa.gov

ANSWERS: 1e, 2b, 3f, 4d, 5g, 6a, 7c, 8h

5 Alone, then pairs

Go through the gapped notes, asking students for the **type** of answer required in each gap. Then students listen again and complete the gaps.

ANSWERS: a scientists, **b** endeavours, **c** astronauts, **d** explorers, **e** radiation, **f** design, **g** materials, **h** detail, **i** www.sciencetomorrow.eur

6 Alone or pairs

For this writing activity, students need to imagine that they are space tourists, taking part in the Da Vinci project (see Did You Know? box), and write a three-day blog that gives information about the three prompts.

G Project work (Coursebook page 80)

For this project, students design a web entry based on an explorer. They can use one from the unit or choose someone different that they know about. First they need to copy and complete the table, then do further research on one of the travellers in order to write their web entry.

Coursebook materials
UNIT 10: What's the best job for a teenager?

Unit introduction

In this unit, the topics are **different jobs past and present**, and the Use of English areas are **direct and reported speech** and **sentence adverbs**.

A Speaking and thinking
(Coursebook page 81)

1/2 Whole class, then pairs

Introduce the topic of jobs and the prompt questions in Activity A1. Get students to work through the questions in pairs, and to prepare a list of the factors that they believe are important when deciding on a suitable job (for a teenager). They can compare their ideas with the list in Activity A2.

3/4 Pairs, then whole class

Students now consider what can make a job interesting or boring. Tell students to think about some people they know and the jobs that they do, and to decide if those jobs are interesting or boring. They should explain their answers. Then they need to make two lists: their top five most interesting and their top five most boring jobs. When students are ready, they can compare their ideas with others in the class. If you have enough time, students could design a graph or chart displaying the information from the discussions.

5 Alone, then pairs

Working alone, students think about the type of job they would like to have in the future. Teenagers often have little or no idea about their future career, so prompt them if necessary. Get them to think about what makes a job attractive to them and to consider whether the ideas from Activity A2 were important or not.

B Reading (Coursebook pages 82–4)

1/2 Pairs, then whole class

Students discuss the jobs in the box (all of which are covered in the reading text on page 83), using paper or digital reference sources if they need help with anything. They must explain which job they think is the best or most interesting, which is the worst

or most boring, and then put them into rank order. Finally, they should compare their order with other pairs in the class.

3 Pairs, then whole class

Students think again about the criteria/factors they used to decide on the best and worst jobs and compare with other pairs in the class.

4 Alone

Working alone, students skim the text about eight jobs and decide if they are 'good' or 'bad' (based on the writer's ideas). They should also check if the text agrees with their own ideas from Activity B2. The words in red and yellow will be dealt with later in this section.

5 Alone, then pairs

Now students focus on the eight red words in the text. They should check the meanings of these adjectives, using paper or digital references sources, then use the adjectives in sentences of their own.

6 Alone, then pairs

The yellow words in the text are all nouns. Students work on their own and match each one with the correct definition a–h. Then they can check with a partner.

ANSWERS: **a** therapy, **b** punishments, **c** gristle, **d** documents, **e** bait, **f** inhabitants, **g** reserve **h** recommendations

7 Alone, then pairs

Before students answer the questions, remind them to underline the key word/s and to think about the type of answer that each question requires. When they have finished writing their answers they can check again with a partner.

ANSWERS:
a by sitting on top of a car
b because traffic jams and parking are not problems for them
c face, nose (for sniffing), arms, elbows, hands (including fingers)
d cleaning and ironing
e in the early evening,
f offer recommendations

8 Pairs, then whole class

Students talk about the eight jobs in the text and decide if they would like to do any of them, giving their reasons. Afterwards, ideas can be shared in class feedback.

C Use of English: Direct and reported speech
(Coursebook pages 84–5)

1 Whole class

Go through the information about direct and reported speech in the blue box, then focus on the activity in the first column (*Look back at the text and find **four** more examples of direct speech*).

ANSWERS:

1 Paragraph 1: A supervisor, Maria Lazarou, tells me: 'This worker has to … a visitor's car.'
2 Paragraph 5: Mathew James … explained that 'Any soldier who … extra guard duty.'
3 Paragraph 7: Dr Jancis Connor … reports: 'In the early evening … . Not much fun!'
4 Paragraph 8: Chris Douglas … . 'We are the good guys,' he claims. 'We are paid … in the future.'

Then get students to make changes to these four examples, putting each one into reported speech.

POSSIBLE ANSWERS:

1 A supervisor, Maria Lazarou, told me that a worker has **or** had to prevent any monkeys from leaving the reserve on the top of a visitor's car.
2 Mathew James, who has just finished one month of guard duty outside the palace, explained **or** explains that any soldier who looked **or** looks less than immaculate was **or** is likely to face a variety of punishments, including extra guard duty.
3 Dr Jancis Connor, a research scientist, reported that in the early evening, when mosquito activity is busiest, they found a mosquito area and set themselves up inside a mosquito-netting tent with a gap at the bottom. The mosquitoes flew in low and got trapped inside, where they were sitting, and they bit them. It was not much fun!
4 Chris Douglas calls himself an 'ethical hacker' or a 'white-hat hacker' and claimed that they were **or** are the good guys. He continued that they were paid to break into a network and to offer their recommendations on how to make sure a real hacker cannot access it in the future.

2 Whole class, then alone

Focus on the picture (but not on the text below it) and ask students if they can guess what Johan Merkel's job is. Then they read the interview to check their predictions. When they have found out Johan's job, they should to rewrite the interview in reported speech, using the words given in blue to start.

SAMPLE ANSWER:

… chief taster in a sweet factory. The interviewer agreed that it was an awesome job and asked Johan how he had got the job. Johan explained that he had seen an advert for a competition in a sports magazine and had decided to enter. After doing this, he had forgotten all about it until he received an email informing him that he had won the competition. The interviewer then wanted to know what Johan had had to do in order to win the competition. Johan told the interviewer that he had said why he liked a particular sweet and had described its flavours. The interviewer's final question was to find out exactly what Johan does in his job. Johan explained that when a new product is planned, he has to taste the first samples and recommend any changes.

DIFFERENTIATED ACTIVITY

For weaker students, provide them with the reporting verbs for each utterance in the interview. You could also provide reported versions of the interviewer's questions, so students need to only report Johan's words.

For stronger students, get them to think of two more questions from the interviewer, and make up two answers from Johan, then continue their report by changing the new questions and answers into reported speech.

D Listening (Coursebook pages 86–7)

1/2 Whole class, then pairs

Get students to think about the man, doctor and child scenario and to discuss who the surgeon is (their relationship is with the child). Most people assume that the surgeon is male, and therefore the surgeon and the man cannot both be the child's father. By thinking laterally ('outside the box'), students should realise that the surgeon is female – the child's **mother**.

3 Pairs

Students make a copy of the table in their notebooks, then complete it with their ideas about jobs. Make sure they understand that this activity is **not** suggesting that some jobs are only for men and others are only for women, but to consider that **traditionally** some jobs were gender-based (for example nursing for women, firefighting for men).

4   Whole class, then alone, then pairs

Prepare students for the audio, making sure they understand who they are going to listen to (a careers counsellor), what they are going to hear (an interview about traditional and non-traditional jobs) and what they have to do (check if the counsellor mentions any of the jobs from Activity D3, and add other jobs to their table). When students are ready, play the audio. They can check their answers with a partner.

TRACK 11

Stefano da Gamo: Hello, everyone, and welcome back to 'Careers Choice'. I'm Stefano da Gamo. In today's programme I'm going to be talking to Véronique Bistoquet, a careers counsellor. Good morning, Véronique, and welcome to our 'Careers Choice' programme.

Véronique Bistoquet: Hello, Stefano.

SdG: We have been talking about male and female jobs. What do you consider to be traditional male and female jobs?

VB: Well, a non-traditional job or career is where more than 75% of the workers are of the opposite gender; or, conversely, where fewer than 25% of the workers are of the same gender.

SdG: So, if we take a traditional male job, say, a firefighter …

VB: Yes?

SdG: If fewer than 25% of the workers are female, that would make it a non-traditional job for females?

VB: Exactly!

SdG: So can you give us some more examples?

VB: Certainly I can. Many non-traditional careers for women fall into rather broad categories – for example, labour-intensive …

SdG: Sorry to interrupt, but what does that mean?

VB: Labour-intensive? Well, a labour-intensive job is one in which there is a lot of physical work – for example, building construction. Also, scientific and technical jobs tend to be for males, rather than females.

SdG: And what about the other way round? Which jobs are more likely to employ women than men?

VB: Unsurprisingly, there are fewer categories here, but education, especially nursery and primary ages, the health industry …

SdG: Yes, nurses are traditionally female, aren't they?

VB: Definitely, although today we are seeing more and more men entering the nursing profession.

SdG: Hmm, that's interesting. So what advice can we give to school-leavers who are considering a non-traditional career? Should they go for it?

VB: Absolutely, although they should also consider the pros and cons.

SdG: Let's start with the bad points, the cons.

VB: Firstly, there may be a lack of people to help you and guide you, and secondly, you may find that the workers of the opposite gender find it difficult to accept you.

SdG: Anything else?

VB: Well, if the job is traditionally male and physical, a female may find this aspect of the job very demanding.

SdG: OK, so what about the advantages, the pros?

VB: Well, the most important thing is that you should follow your dreams, as far as possible! If a woman wants to be a builder, then why shouldn't she?

SdG: For sure!

VB: Next, people of the opposite gender tend to get more attention from other workers …

SdG: But can't that be a disadvantage as well?

VB: Yes, if it's not dealt with in the right way, but positive attention can lead to bigger and better things.

SdG: I see. Anything else?

VB: I think, for our society in the 21st century, it is important for all jobs to be accessible to people of both genders. If we lock the door, society will not move forward.

SdG: A very interesting point to finish on. Thanks again for joining us today, Véronique Bistoquet.

5   Alone, then pairs

Play the audio again. This time students make notes about the advantages and disadvantages of choosing a non-traditional career, then check with their partner.

ANSWERS:

Advantages	Disadvantages
Following your dreams	Lack of help and
Often more attention	guidance
from other workers	Opposite gender may
Society moves forward	not accept you
when gender is not a	Could be physically
problem	demanding

6 Pairs

Students work together to try to remember the answers to four of the questions from the interview.

ANSWERS:

a more than 75% of workers are of opposite gender / fewer than 25% same gender
b lot of physical work
c education (nursery/primary), health care
d yes, but should consider pros and cons

7 Alone

Refer students to the audioscript on page 154 to check their notes from Activity D5. Then they use their notes in order to write two short paragraphs: one about the advantages and one about the disadvantages of choosing a non-traditional career.

8 Pairs

Students interview each other, taking the roles of careers counsellor and student. They should use language and ideas from the unit. If you have the facilities for students to record themselves, this is a great way to give them feedback on their performance.

E Use of English: Sentence adverbs (Coursebook page 87)

1/2 Whole class, then pairs, then alone

Focus on the information about sentence adverbs in the green box, then get students to think about the meaning of the seven adverbs a–g. When they are ready, students work alone to use five of the adverbs in sentences of their own.

F Writing (Coursebook pages 87–8)

1 Pairs

Students work together and think about the questions they might ask when applying for a part-time job. Focus on the two examples given to get them started. Other questions could be:

Do I have to wear a uniform?
Will I be working alone or with other people?
Is the job outside or inside?
Can I have extra hours during the holidays?
Do I get more money if I work at the weekends?

2 Pairs

When students have a list of questions ready, they take on the roles of applicant and prospective employer (the new boss). During the interview, the applicant needs to make a note of the boss's answers to the questions.

3 Alone

After the interview, students write an article about it for their school's web page, reporting all the information about the new part-time job.

G Project work (Coursebook page 88)

This project is about jobs from many years ago. Students need to do some research about three of the five jobs mentioned in the table, then select one as the basis for a PowerPoint presentation.

Coursebook materials
UNIT 11: Who are the Maasai?

Unit introduction

In this unit, the topics are **running, sports** and **Maasai warriors**, and the Use of English areas are **word building** and **-ing forms**.

A Speaking and thinking
(Coursebook page 89)

1 **Whole class**
Introduce the topic and, if you think that students won't know much about the Maasai, you could show them a visual to help them make some predictions.

2 **Pairs, then whole class**
Students now consider the topic of marathons and marathon runners, and discuss the prompt questions.

3/4 **Pairs**
Working together, students look at statements a–f and decide if they are true or false. They will find out later in the unit, so there is no need to tell them yet if they are right or wrong. Students also need to say if they found any of the pieces of information surprising, and give their reasons.

5/6 **Pairs**
Students continue their discussion. This time they talk about sports shoes and answer questions a–c in Activity A5 and the questions about women and men in A6.

B Reading (Coursebook pages 90–1)

1 **Whole class, then pairs**
Ask students to tell you (or make a list) of what situations sports shoes are manufactured for, such as playing tennis, marathon running, and so on. Then get them to think about other factors people should consider when buying sports shoes (apart from the situation in which they are going to use them) – for example price and size.

2 **Whole class**
Introduce the words *arch*, *sole*, *heel* and *ball*, asking students to show you where on the foot each of

these is. A diagram on the board is probably the best way to do this.

3/4 **Pairs**
Let students look at the information and diagrams about the 'wet test', making sure they understand what it is, then get them to match the instructions to the pictures in Activity B4.
ANSWERS: 1D, 2A, 3C, 4B

5 **Whole class, then alone**
Go through the information about *pronation*, and point out the three foot diagrams in blue to the left of the activities. Students skim the text and match the three diagrams to the three runners.
ANSWERS: Marios = top, Nektarios = bottom left, Stelios = bottom right

6 **Alone**
Students work alone to find the words in the text that match the definitions a–j.
ANSWERS: a contrary to popular belief, b collapses, c absorbs, d stability, e entire, f resulting in, g excessive, h motion, i firmer, j vital

DIFFERENTIATED ACTIVITY

For weaker students, you could allocate fewer words to different students, and/or tell them in which paragraph to look for the answers.
For stronger students, because the list of meanings is in the same order as the words in the text, you could provide students with a revised list – the same meanings but jumbled up (ie, not in the same order as the words in the text).

7 **Alone, then pairs**
Before students answer the questions, remind them to underline the key word/s and to think about the type of answer that each question requires. When they have finished writing their answers they can check again with a partner.
ANSWERS:
a because it absorbs shock
b stability shoe with moderate arch support
c arch collapses too much, increased risk of injuries

d stability have midsoles and supports, motion have firmer support

e if you just see the heel and a thin outside line of the foot

f supinator

g too much shock travelling up the leg

C Use of English: Word building
(Coursebook pages 91–2)

1 Whole class, then alone, then pairs
Go through the information about word building in the blue box, then focus on Activity C1. Students need to copy the table and fill in as many of the gaps as possible. They can check with a partner after they have filled in the table.

ANSWERS:

Verb	Noun	Adjective	Adverb
	common	common	commonly
absorbs	absorption	absorbent	
provides	provision, provider		
	entirety	entire	entirely
exceed	excess	excessive	excessively
stabilise	stability, stable	stable	
	severity	severe	severely
encourage	encouragement	encouraged	encouragingly

2 Pairs
Now students work together to remember as much as they can about the text *Choosing your shoes*. They need to tell each other about the three types of arches: normal, flat and high.

D Listening and writing
(Coursebook pages 92–3)

1/2 Whole class, then pairs
Go through the information about the Maasai before getting students to work together to discuss and answer the questions in Activities D1 and D2. They will find out the answers during the listening activity.

3/4 Whole class, then pairs
Prepare students for the audio by checking that they understand who they are going to listen to (a reporter), what they are going to hear (information about the Maasai warriors and their participation in the London marathon) and what they have to do

while listening (check their answers to Activity D3). Before they listen, students decide if statements a–g are true or false (they are all true). Then play the audio and, as students listen, they check their predictions about the statements.

TRACK 12

Announcer: Last week, our reporter Jemima Freebody was lucky enough to meet a group of Maasai warriors who were preparing to run in the London marathon. Here is her report.

Jemima Freebody: The Maasai often run for days and nights without stopping, with shoes made from car tyres, cut up and strapped to their feet, so taking part in the London marathon was no problem for the six Maasai warriors who went to the UK from their village of Eluai, in northern Tanzania, as part of a campaign to raise money to find a vital water source.

The Maasai warriors, all between 20 and 25 years old, expected to finish the marathon race in less than four and a half hours. Running in traditional dress – a red blanket toga and car-tyre sandals – they carried spears and shields showing their race numbers. Before the race, they said that they sometimes run for five or six days, day and night, eating only twice a day, and with no water.

The Maasai warriors hoped to raise enough money to find and access a fresh water source for their community, something which could cost up to €75,000. In fact, after the race, they had raised nearly double that amount.

Years of drought around Eluai is killing the cattle and threatening their way of life with disease and famine. Two-thirds of the children born, die before they reach the age of five. The village is quite large, but has a severe lack of water, with only one water source, which runs out quickly and which is often not clean.

Ground surveys of the area around Eluai have found an underground water source which could offer the Maasai a lifeline. The procedure for extracting water is enormously complex and expensive, but the need is desperate.

---

5 Alone, then pairs
Students listen to the audio for a second time and complete the notes. When they have finished, they compare their answers with a partner. You can also refer them to the audioscript on page 155 to check their answers.

ANSWERS:
a stopping
b (i) Eluai, (ii) Tanzania
c (i) 20–25, (ii) less than 4.5
d (i) toga, (ii) car-tyre, (iii) spears, (iv) shields
e 75,000
f drought
g five

6 Alone
Using the information they have obtained in this section, students write a short paragraph about the Maasai warriors and their visit to London.

E Use of English: *-ing* forms
(Coursebook page 93)

1 Whole class, then pairs
Focus on the information about *-ing* forms in the green box, then get students in pairs to think about the words printed in blue (*running*) in Activity E1 and whether the word *running* is a verb, noun, adverb or adjective in each sentence a–d.

ANSWERS: a adjective, **b** verb, **c** noun, **d** adverb

2 Alone, then pairs
Working alone, students complete the sentences a–h in their notebooks with the *-ing* form of the verb given in brackets. Then they need to decide if the *-ing* form is a verb, noun, adverb or adjective.

ANSWERS: a smoking (noun), **b** eating (verb), **c** talking (noun), **d** crying (adverb), **e** winding (adjective), **f** singing (verb), **g** dressing (verb), **h** knowing (verb)

F Reading and writing
(Coursebook pages 94–6)

1/2 Whole class, then pairs
Introduce the idea of 'unusual' sports, perhaps by immediately focusing on the pictures in Activity F2, in which students match the pictures to the four sports in the box. Ask students what makes a sport unusual, using the prompts in Activity F1.

ANSWERS: 1 = underwater rugby, 2 = tuna-throwing, 3 = land-diving, 4 = swamp football

3/4 Alone, then pairs
Quickly check for any vocabulary problems. Students should then work alone to decide which of the four sports matches the phrases in the box. They should try to give reasons. Afterwards, they skim the four texts on page 95 to check their predictions, and compare their ideas with a partner.

ANSWERS:
underwater rugby: *swimming pool, there are no normal rules*
tuna-throwing: *in excess of 50 kilograms, the weight of a grown adult*
land-diving: *bungee jumping, their legs tied*
swamp football: *without sinking, very physically demanding*

5 Pairs
Students work together to answer questions a–g.
ANSWERS: a land-diving, **b** underwater rugby, **c** underwater rugby and swamp football, **d** tuna-throwing, **e** underwater rugby and swamp football, **f** land-diving, **g** tuna-throwing

6 Pairs
Students look at four more unusual sports and predict what they think happens in each one. They should make a copy of the table in their notebooks and add any information they find, using paper or digital reference sources. Then they choose one of the four sports and write a short description of it. This can be a shared writing activity.

7 Pairs
Working with a partner again, students think about an unusual sport in their own country, or any other unusual sport that they know about. They need to write a description of the sport, using the question prompts and including a picture or diagram if possible.

G Project work (Coursebook page 96)
For this project, students design an information leaflet about the Maasai warriors, using information they research themselves and including pictures and other visuals.

45

Unit introduction

In this unit, the topic is **sports**, and the Use of English areas are **sentence patterns with comparatives**, **'signpost' words** and **future forms**.

A Speaking and thinking
(Coursebook pages 97–8)

1 Pairs, then whole class
Introduce the topic and then put students in pairs to work through questions a–e. They can make notes during their discussion to use during class feedback. Monitor the discussions, but do not interfere, allowing students plenty of freedom to talk without fear of correction or interruption. Be positive about their efforts during feedback, and only pick up on any serious language errors that you feel need attention.

2/3 Pairs
Students now think about the three sports they discussed in Activity A1e – swimming, cycling and running – and agree which of the pieces of sports equipment in the box match each sport. They will find out the answers when they read the text in the next section. They should also explain what they think the pieces of equipment are important for – for example goggles are important for keeping water out of a swimmer's eyes.

4 Pairs
Working together, students think of two other pieces of equipment that might be useful for each of the three sports.

B Reading (Coursebook pages 98–9)

1 Whole class
Go through the information in Activity B1 and see if students can give you the word *triathlete* for an athlete who competes in three different sports.

2 Pairs
In this matching activity, students work with a partner. They need to decide which of the pieces of sports equipment a–h are associated with the 16 phrases. It does not matter at this stage if they are unsure, but they should try to give a reason for their

choices. Some phrases may match more than one piece of equipment (for example *a good fit* works with wetsuit, goggles and shoes).

3 Alone
Students skim the text and check if their choices from Activity B2 were correct.

4 Alone, then pairs
Before students answer the questions, remind them to find the key word/s and to think about the type of answer that each question requires. When they have written their answers they can check with a partner.

ANSWERS:
a not flexible, body movement difficult (because made of thick material)
b mask-type
c it will not give good protection
d can be worn under wetsuit, so immediately ready for next event
e price
f ultra-lightweight trainers
g protect soft feet
h an HRM

C Use of English: Sentence patterns with comparatives
(Coursebook pages 100–1)

1 Whole class, then alone, then pairs
Go through the information about sentence patterns with comparatives in the blue box, then focus on Activity C1. Students need to decide what has not been mentioned in each question. They should compare their decisions with a partner.

ANSWERS: a than cheap wetsuits, **b** small goggles, **c** than the cheaper ones, **d** than the basic ones

2 Whole class, then alone
In this activity, students need to write a comparison of the two products shown: TRX Force Kit and XFIT Rings. Depending on their level, you could allow students to use paper or digital reference sources to check the meaning of any difficult vocabulary, or go through the vocabulary together as a class. When students are ready, they can use the product information in the table to write their comparison.

3 Pairs, then whole class

Working together, students make a list of all the 'signpost' words they can remember. You could combine ideas from different pairs to make one class list.

4 Alone, then pairs

Students read sentences a–e and identify the 'signpost' word/s in each one, then compare answers with a partner.

ANSWERS: **a** but, and, **b** and, such as, **c** Furthermore, **d** In addition, and, **e** However

5 Alone, then pairs

For this activity, students need to rewrite the sentences from Activity C4, replacing the 'signpost' words with suitable alternatives. There are several possibilities, so be prepared for students to come up with different answers. For example: *Although/ While you can buy quite cheap wetsuits these days, the problem is that they tend to be of quite thick material and are not very flexible, making body movements quite difficult.* Or *You can buy quite cheap wetsuits these days. However, the problem is that they tend to be of quite thick material and are not very flexible, making body movements quite difficult.*

D Listening (Coursebook pages 101–2)

1/2 Whole class, then pairs

Prepare students for the audio by checking that they understand who they are going to listen to (a triathlete from Malawi, Sambulo Mbeya), what they are going to hear (an interview about triathletes) and what they have to do while listening (check their answers to Activities D1 and D2). Before they listen, students decide which of the words and phrases in the box they think they will hear. Then, for Activity D2, they read questions a–e and predict the answers.

3 Alone, then pairs

Students listen to the audio and check which of the words and phrases from Activity D1 are spoken (they all are). When they have finished, they compare their answers with a partner.

TRACK 13

Towera Mzimba: I'm Towera Mzimba and my special guest on today's show is Sambulo Mbeya, our very own athlete! Hello Sambulo and welcome back to today's show.

Sambulo Mbeya: Thanks for inviting me again, Towera.

TM: As the triathlon season is coming up, let's return to your favourite sport. Last month, you told our listeners about the equipment they need. What are you going to talk about today?

SM: Well, it doesn't matter how good your equipment is, time is the most important aspect for the triathlete.

TM: What do you mean, exactly?

SM: Remember that there are three events, each one held immediately after the other, so it is vital for the transition between swimming, cycling and running to be as smooth and as fast as possible.

TM: Is it possible to improve your position against the other athletes?

SM: Yes, for sure, but only if you have a safe technique during the transitions.

TM: So, what's the technique to improve your time?

SM: You need baby oil, talcum powder and Vaseline®!

TM: You're joking, right?

SM: No, I'm not. If you apply baby oil around your shoulders, arms and ankles before putting on your wetsuit, it can help save precious minutes – otherwise the wetsuit can get stuck to your body.

TM: That makes a lot of sense. Where does the talcum powder go?

SM: Inside your cycling shoes, which should, of course, be already clipped to the bike pedals. Talcum powder will help your wet feet slide in more easily.

TM: OK, and the Vaseline®?

SM: This is for your running shoes, inside the shoes, at points where the shoes rub against your feet. This means you won't need to wear socks.

TM: Well, it all makes very good sense. Any other advice you can give, to help our triathletes to save time?

SM: A good tip is to have elastic laces on your shoes, so you don't have to tie knots with wet, slippery fingers after the swimming event. Also, if you wear a trisuit under your wetsuit, this means that you won't have to waste time putting on shorts and a T-shirt before commencing the bike race.

TM: How much time can be saved?

SM: Put everything together and the total could come to around five minutes. It's far easier to save time in this way than to save the time during the events themselves.

TM: Thanks again for coming in today, Sambulo, and good luck during the triathlon season which starts very soon!

SM: Thanks very much.

Adapted from 'Survival Kit', *The Independent on Sunday*.

4   Alone, then pairs

Students listen again and check what Sambulo says in response to the questions in Activity D2. Then they check with a partner.

ANSWERS: a yes, **b** use baby oil, talcum powder and Vaseline, **c** inside shoes, **d** elastic laces on shoes, wear trisuit under wetsuit, **e** around five minutes

E   Use of English: Future forms
(Coursebook pages 102–3)

1/2   Whole class, then pairs

Focus on the information about future forms in the green box, then get students in pairs to copy and complete the table in Activity E1. They will see possible answers in Activity E2.

3   Alone, then pairs

Students read the text on their own and put the verbs in brackets a–g into the correct future form. In some cases, more than one future form may be possible. Allow students some time to check their answers with a partner.

ANSWERS: a travel, **b** are looking ahead, **c** will be awarded, **d** meet/s, **e** will compete, **f** are fighting, **g** are knocking

F   Reading and writing
(Coursebook pages 103–4)

1   Whole class, then pairs

Go through the instructions carefully and find out if students know anything about the two different sports they are going to read about: the Mayan 'ball game' and fishermen's jousting. Before students read their texts, they need to prepare eight questions to ask each other, using the words given in a–i (for example *Where is the sport played? / Where do people play the sport?*) Give them sufficient time to write their questions, and check for accuracy.

DIFFERENTIATED ACTIVITY

For weaker students, let them work with a partner to write the questions in Activity F1. Also, you could supply more help for the questions (for example *Where / people / play / sport?*) Another option is to divide up the questions among students so that they only need to write two or three each. Then they can share their questions.

For stronger students, provide question words only so they have to form their questions without the help of any other words. You could also remove all support and tell them that they need to think of six to eight questions to ask their partner about their sport.

2   Alone, then A/B pairs

Put students into A/B Pairs. Student A reads the text about the Mayan 'ball game' while Student B reads about fishermen's jousting. When they have finished reading, students take it in turns to ask each other their questions from Activity F1 and take notes of their partner's answers (they will need this in the next activity).

3   Alone

Students work alone and write a short comparison of the two sports, using the information they collected in Activity F2 from their partner, as well as comparative forms they studied in Section C. When they have finished, they should read their partner's text and check if there is anything they can add to their piece of writing.

G   Project work (Coursebook page 104)

For this project, students do some research on sports, recording the information in a copy of the table in Activity G1, and then choose one sport as the basis for an oral presentation.

Coursebook materials
UNIT 13: How much water do you use?

Unit introduction

In this unit, the topics are **science and scientists**, **Leonardo da Vinci** and **water**, and the Use of English areas are **the passive** and **word building**.

A Speaking and thinking
(Coursebook page 105)

1 Pairs
Introduce the topic and then get students to work through questions a–d in pairs. They should make notes that they can then use during class feedback. Monitor, but do not interfere during the discussions, allowing students plenty of freedom to talk without fear of correction or interruption. Be positive about their efforts during feedback, and only pick up on any serious language errors that you feel need attention.

2/3 Pairs
Students may recognise some of the words in the box but others may be unfamiliar, so allow them to use paper or digital reference sources to check any that they are unsure of. Encourage students to think of equivalent words in their own language. In Activity A3, students should copy the table and categorise the words, giving reasons where possible.

ANSWERS:

Physics	Chemistry	Other
force	reaction	biology
atoms	elements	science
gravity	compounds	
magnetism		
electricity		

4 Pairs
Working together, students copy and complete the two definitions.
ANSWERS: a Chemistry, **b** Physics

5 Pairs
Using the two definitions from the previous activity as a model, students discuss what they think biology is, then fill in gaps a–e in the definition, using the words in the box.
ANSWERS: a life, **b** organisms, **c** cell, **d** plants, **e** animals

B Reading (Coursebook pages 106–7)

1/2 Alone, then pairs
There are eight scientific definitions for students to read. Each definition has one word removed, which students need to find in the box at the start of the activity. When they have done this, they match each paragraph to one of the pictures at the bottom of the page.
ANSWERS:
(B1): i elements, **ii** compounds, **iii** reactions, **iv** force, **v** gravity, **vi** magnetism, **vii** electricity, **viii** atoms
(B2): clockwise from left – elements (A), atoms (H), electricity (G), force (D), compounds (B), reactions (C), magnetism (F), gravity (E)

DIFFERENTIATED ACTIVITY

For weaker students, allocate fewer definitions. You could, for example, split the weaker students into two groups and give one group paragraphs A–D and the other group paragraphs E–H. An alternative approach is to complete Activity B1 for students, and ask them to focus on matching the pictures to the paragraphs (Activity B2).

For stronger students, remove the list of words in Activity B1 so that they have to think of the missing words in each paragraph. Alternatively, supply more words than the eight needed, to act as distractors.

3/4 Pairs
Students focus on the six verbs in the box in Activity B3 and the five nouns in Activity B4 (all taken from the paragraphs they have just read). Using paper or digital reference sources they need to check what the verbs and nouns mean, then think of equivalent words in their own language.

5 Alone, then pairs

Before students answer the questions, remind them to find the key word/s and to think about the type of answer that each question requires. When they have written their answers, they can check with a partner.

ANSWERS:

a around 22

b from elements combining

c when new substances are formed from existing ones

d it receives an equal and opposite force in return

e the moon's gravity

f similar poles repel each other, opposite poles attract

g by the movement of invisible particles

h protons and neutrons

C Use of English: The passive

(Coursebook pages 107–8)

1 Whole class, then alone, then pairs

Go through the information about the passive in the blue box and help students complete the definition using the words provided. Then get them to refer to the text in Section B and find at least eight more examples of passive forms. They can check with a partner at the end.

ANSWERS:

(Box): a person, b thing, c action, d person, e thing, f performs, g doer

(C1): *is made up of, are said, are produced, is made up of, are created, is created, are ignited, are used, is known, are surrounded, is used, is made up of*

2 Whole class, then pairs

If you think students may struggle to discuss Leonardo da Vinci, provide some pictures to act as prompts, then move on to Activity C3.

3 Alone, then pairs

Students work alone to read the text about Leonardo da Vinci and to put the verbs a–g into the correct tense. Remind them that four verbs should be in the past, two in the present perfect and one in the past perfect. When they are ready they can check their answers with a partner.

ANSWERS:

a was ever convinced

b were built

c were never published

d were discovered

e had been built

f have been revolutionised

g have been constructed

4 Pairs, then whole class

Working together, students answer questions a–d.

ANSWERS:

a nobody would pay for them **or** da Vinci lost interest in them

b many years after his death

c if da Vinci's machines had been built

d some have been constructed

D Listening (Coursebook pages 108–9)

1/2 Whole class, then pairs

Prepare students for the audio by checking that they understand who they are going to listen to (a scientist, Vanessa Woo), what they are going to hear (an interview about water) and what they have to do while listening (make notes about Vanessa's answers to the interviewer's questions). Before they listen, students write the questions that Vanessa is asked by the interviewer, using the words and phrases provided. All the questions are in the present tense. One example is given.

ANSWERS:

b Is water all around us?

c Why do we need water?

d How much water do we need?

e What would happen if we didn't get enough water?

f How can we make sure that we get enough water?

g How serious is the global water shortage problem?

h How can we save water?

2 Pairs

Now students predict the answers to the questions from the previous activity.

3 Pairs

Students look at the words and phrases in the box and predict which ones they will hear during the interview, giving their reasons (all the words and phrases appear in the interview).

4 Alone, then pairs

Students listen to the audio and make notes about Vanessa's answers, checking for differences with their predictions in Activity D2.

TRACK 14

Jackie Lee: Our science programme today concentrates on something we all take very much for granted, but which we cannot do without. Can you guess what it is? Let's talk to Vanessa Woo and find out … Hello, Vanessa, and welcome to our weekly science programme.

Vanessa Woo: Hi, Jackie. What's our topic today?

JL: Water! What exactly is water?

VW: Hmm, an interesting question. Water is the liquid form of the chemical H_2O. There are two atoms of hydrogen (that's the H_2) and one atom of oxygen (that's the O) in every molecule of water.

JL: Ah, so that's what that wet stuff is!

VW: Well, yes and no. There's a lot of liquid water about – it covers about 70% of the earth's surface. But water can also be a solid or a gas, so it's not always wet!

JL: Solid water I understand – if you freeze it, you get ice. But when is water a gas?

VW: If water is heated to 100 degrees centigrade, so that it boils, you get steam, or water vapour.

JL: Oh yes, of course! Vanessa, is water all around us?

VW: Yes, it is. About 97% of the water on the earth's surface is in the world's oceans. The other 3% is in lakes, rivers, at the polar ice caps, in the clouds, falling as rain, or it is stored in rocks. And don't forget sea ice, such as icebergs!

JL: But why is water so important? Why do we need it so badly?

VW: Well, all living creatures need water to survive. A human being can live without water for only a few days at most and we may last only a few hours. The problem is that we are constantly losing water from our bodies. Things like breathing and digesting food to make energy use up water and, of course, we sweat and pass urine. Water has to be replaced by eating and drinking.

JL: How much water do we need?

VW: Well, about 70% of a person's weight is water – so quite a lot! Depending on your lifestyle, you might need anywhere between 1 and 7 litres a day. If you have a physically demanding job, you will need more than someone who sits at a desk all day. Climate is also a factor, especially temperature.

JL: What happens if we don't get enough water?

VW: Simple – you become dehydrated. This can cause serious health problems, such as kidney damage, but even mild dehydration can be unpleasant – you might feel tired, headachy and unable to concentrate.

JL: So how can we get enough water?

VW: The best thing to do is make drinking water part of your routine, so that you do it without thinking about it. Drink a glass of water when you wake up and carry a bottle of water with you when you go out. Eating fresh fruit and vegetables will help too.

JL: How serious is the global water shortage problem?

VW: It is more than serious – the world is in crisis as far as water is concerned. Up to 2 million children in the developing world die every year because they don't have access to clean water or a proper sanitation system. They have to drink or cook with dirty water, and there are no sinks and toilets connected to proper sanitation systems. It is dreadful that in the 21st century, people are still dying of poor hygiene.

JL: I agree. So, how can we all save water?

VW: Very simply. One of the best things you can do is give up baths. A five-minute shower uses only a third of the water you would need for a bath, so you could save up to 400 litres a week by showering instead. And don't run the tap while you're brushing your teeth – rinsing your mouth out from a glass of water instead saves around 12 litres each time.

JL: Great advice Vanessa. Is there anything our parents should be doing as well?

VW: If they have a garden, they could get a water butt. Rainwater collects in the barrel, and you can then use it for watering plants. Speaking of plants, if you have a fish tank, you can collect the dirty water and use it as a fertiliser – it's rich in nitrogen and phosphorus.

JL: Vanessa, thanks once again for visiting us.

5   **Alone, then pairs**
Play the audio again for students to check which of the words and phrases from Activity D3 are spoken (they all are) and in what order.

ANSWERS: H_2O, freeze, water vapour, polar ice caps, sweat, weight, temperature, health problems, fruit and vegetables, sinks and toilets, poor hygiene, 400 litres, brushing your teeth, fish tank

6   **Pairs, then whole class**
The section finishes with a short discussion about water in the students' own country and whether or not there is a water problem. Students can discuss this topic in pairs, then give feedback to the whole class.

E Use of English: Word building
(Coursebook page 110)

1 Alone, then pairs
Working on their own, students copy and complete the table with the words in the box, then fill in the gaps in the table. When they have finished, they can check with a partner.
ANSWERS:

Verb	Noun	Adjective	Adverb
discover	discovery	discovered	
differ	difference	different	differently
include	inclusion	including	inclusively
combine	combination	combined	
react	reactions	reactive	reactively
exerts	exertion	exerted	
attract	attraction	attractive	attractively
power	power	powerful	powerfully
depend	dependence, dependent	dependable	dependently
replace	replacement	replaced	
shorten	shortage	short	shortly

2 Alone
Students choose at least seven words (you can vary this depending on the level your students are working at) from their completed table to use in sentences of their own.

F Reading and writing
(Coursebook pages 110–12)

1 Alone, then pairs
Students think about how much water they use on a regular basis and whether or not they waste water. They should make a list of how they use water inside and outside the house, for example rinsing fruit before eating it, washing the car. They should then compare their lists with a partner.

2/3 Pairs
Students are going to read a text about a washing machine that uses very little water. Before they read, they need to consider if this is actually possible and then decide if the statements in Activity F2 are true or false. They will find out when they read the text.

4 Alone
Students skim the text and check their predictions from Activity F3 (all the statements are true).

5 Alone, then pairs
Students work alone to find words or phrases in the text that are similar the ones given. They can check their answers with a partner.
ANSWERS: a conventional, **b** drawback, **c** chips, **d** stains, **e** virtually, **f** get rid of, **g** astonishing, **h** tiny, **i** renewable

6 Whole class, then alone
Go through the instructions for the writing activity carefully, making sure that students understand the process. They should make notes first of all, responding to the prompt questions, then think about how to write their email. As they are writing it to a friend, the style should be informal. Students can include pictures or diagrams in their email if they wish.

G Project work (Coursebook page 112)

There are three things for students to do in this project. First they do some bilingual vocabulary work. Then they complete a copy of the table by researching three of the water machines/uses. Finally they use this information to make a PowerPoint presentation about one of the water machines.

Coursebook materials
UNIT 14: How important is oil?

Unit introduction

In this unit, the topics are **oil, plastic, mobile phones** and **inventions and discoveries**, and the Use of English areas are **question forms** and **time references with different tenses**.

A Speaking and thinking
(Coursebook page 113)

1 **Whole class, then pairs**
Introduce the topic, then put students in pairs to work through questions a–c. You could allocate the three questions to three different groups to save time. If you do this, make sure you do class feedback so that everyone has a chance to hear the different opinions.

2 **Pairs**
Set a time limit for pairs to make a list of products they believe are made from oil. If they struggle with this, point out that the five pictures on page 113 are all examples (but students cannot use them in their lists!). Or you could ask for a list of ten oil-based products and see which pair of students finishes first.

3 **Pairs, then whole class**
Working together, students discuss the questions. Do not worry if they are unsure, as they will find out more about plastic later in the unit.

4 **Pairs, then whole class**
Students talk about how important each of the items pictured is in their lives. Students should also discuss which three items they think they could not live without, giving reasons and asking other students for their ideas.

B Reading (Coursebook pages 113–16)

1/2/3 **Alone, then A/B pairs**
Students are going to read two versions (A and B) of the same text. There are five different pieces of information missing from each version. Each student needs to read their text and prepare five questions to ask their partner in order to find out the missing information. As they ask and answer, students

make a note of their partner's responses. Finally, students read their partner's text and check the notes they made.

POSSIBLE ANSWERS:
Student A's questions:
a Who was the Belgian chemist?
b Where did he emigrate to?
c What was the result of his experiments?
d When did Baekeland die?
e How many barrels of oil a day do plastics account for?

Student B's questions:
a When did he write in his diary?
b How long did Baekeland spend experimenting (in his New York home)?
c How many years has it been since Bakelite was invented?
d How much plastic was the USA producing each year when Baekeland died?
e Where is the use of plastic still rising by 4% per year?

Student B's answers to Student A's questions:
a Leo Hendrick Baekeland, b America, c a hard, light substance (that could take on any shape), d 1944, e 7 million

Student A's answers to Student B's questions:
a 11th July 1907, b five years, c over 100, d 400,000 tonnes, e the UK

4 **Alone, then whole class**
Students work alone to find words or phrases in the text that match a–j. If time is short, or to help weaker students, you could allocate fewer questions and then bring everyone together to share their ideas

ANSWERS: a extent, b emigrated, c oven, d synthetic, e moulded, f rocketed, g decades, h ivory, i versatility, j widespread

5 **Alone, then pairs**
Before students answer the questions, remind them to find the key word/s first and to think about the type of answer that each question requires. When they have written their answers they can check with a partner.

ANSWERS:
a 3
b he called it the material of a thousand uses

c 400,000 = tonnes of plastic produced annually in USA when B died, 100 million = tonnes in 2010, 60,000 = two-litre drink bottles being produced every second

d because oil reserves are running out

e lack versatility, expensive, melt at low temperatures

6 Whole class
Get students to look back at the questions they came up with in Activity B1 and elicit the answer that these are *wh-* question forms.

C Use of English: Question forms (Coursebook page 116)

1 Whole class, then pairs
Go through the information about question forms in the blue box, then put students in pairs to complete the questions in Activity A1. They may come up with variations on the answers listed below, particularly with the tenses.

POSSIBLE ANSWERS:

a What is the car called?

b How much does it cost?

c Where/How is it made?

d When is it available?

e Who invented it?

f What does it look like?

g Why/How is it so economical?

h Who will use the new car?

i Where is the car produced?

j How is the car powered?

D Reading (Coursebook pages 116–18)

1/2 Pairs, then alone
Students work together to predict the answers to the multiple-choice questions a–e. When they are ready, they skim the text to check their predictions.

ANSWERS: a 1960s, b all of these, c 1983, d a briefcase, e all of these

3 Alone, then pairs
Before students read the text again and answer the questions, remind them to find the key word/s first and to think about the type of answer that each question requires. When they have written their answers they can check with a partner.

ANSWERS:

a yes – text says 'in one form or another'

b less reliable, more static, more noise interference

c no – not very mobile and very large, expensive

d faster and quieter

e no – text says *created very soon after...*

f can transfer voice data, emails, visual information and instant messages

g high-speed Internet

h no – because of growing needs

E Use of English: Time references with different tenses (Coursebook page 118)

1 Whole class, then alone
Go through the information about time references with different tenses in the blue box, then put students in pairs and get them to refer back to the text on mobile phones to find five more examples of time references.

ANSWERS:

Paragraph 1: for the last 20 years or so (present perfect), since the 1960s (present perfect), today's (future in the past), in the late 1940s (past), then (past), first (past)

Paragraph 2: in 1983 (past), today (present)

Paragraph 3: during this era (past), After a few years (past)

Paragraph 4: During the 1990s (past)

Paragraph 5: today (present), over the past 20–25 years (present perfect)

Paragraph 6: in the early 21st century (present), now (present), before (present)

Paragraph 7: since the 1990s (present perfect), a mere 30 years ago (past)

F Listening (Coursebook pages 118–19)

1 Pairs
Students think about the difference between an *invention* and a *discovery*. If they are unsure, give them some examples. For example Bakelite was an invention, but the continent of America was a discovery made by Europeans (even though people already lived there).

2/3 Pairs
Students look at the list of inventions in the box, and guess when each one was invented. Then they make a copy of the timeline on page 119 and match the inventions to the correct year.

ANSWERS: bow and arrow, pottery, wheel, glass, lock and key, knitting, eye glasses, pocket watch, contact lenses

3 Alone, then pairs
Prepare students for the audio by checking that they understand who they are going to listen to

(a scientist), what they are going to hear (a talk about inventions through the ages) and what they have to do while listening (check their answers to Activity F2). After they have listened to the audio, they can check their answers with a partner.

TRACK 15

One of the earliest-known inventions is the bow and arrow, which is still used throughout the world today, 15,000 years after it was first invented. Of course, these days, the bow and arrow is used mainly in sporting events, but in some places it is still a means of killing animals for food.

In western Asia, another extremely important invention was born – the ability to produce pots. As long as 6500 years ago, people were producing pottery, mostly plain and without designs, but the technique has changed little since.

Some people say that the wheel is the single most important invention. Early examples from about 5000 years ago have been found in the forests of Europe. Around 1500 years later, the Phoenicians used sand, limestone and sodium carbonate to produce something else which we would be lost without – glass.

How many things do you lock with a key every day? Doors, cupboards? The car? We really don't think much about them, do we? Well, the first example of a lock and key dates back to 2750 years ago, in Assyria. This is a lock on a large wooden door in the palace of Sargon II.

Another amazing invention, which we probably take for granted these days, is the skill of knitting, which first appeared in the Roman Empire, some 1700 years ago. The earliest examples are knitted socks!

Eye glasses developed from just one lens in a frame, like a simple magnifying glass, way back in the 13th century. In about 1290, the idea to put two lenses in a frame to sit on the nose was developed in Florence. And, believe it or not, the modern contact lens is 120 years old!

Time flies and we spend a lot of time checking how much time we have left! This would be impossible without clocks and watches, which are all around us: on walls, on our wrists, on our PCs, and even on our mobiles and iPod®s. The first pocket watch was invented by Thomas Tompion (1639–1714) in England 330 years ago, and his watch-face design, with two (and sometimes three) hands moving around a single dial, has remained largely unchanged in all that time.

---

4   **Pairs**
Working together, students discuss what they think is the world's greatest invention, if anybody from their own country has invented anything and if there is an invention that has changed their lives in a significant way.

5   **Alone**
Students use their ideas from the previous activity to write an article for their school magazine, which can include pictures or diagrams if they wish.

G Project work (Coursebook page 119)

There are three things for students to do in this project. First they research three of their favourite pieces of technology and record the information they find in a copy of the table. Then they focus on one of the items and consider how it could be improved. Finally they make a presentation to the class. Students can choose how they present their findings, but they should include pictures and other visuals where possible.

Coursebook materials

UNIT 15: How do you say 'bridge' in your language?

Unit introduction

In this unit, the topics are **bridges**, **the Icehotel** and **the city of Atlantis**, and the Use of English areas are **verbs ending in** *-en* and **intensifying adjectives**.

A Speaking and thinking
(Coursebook pages 120–1)

1/2 Whole class, then pairs
Introduce the topic, then pair up students to think about the English word *bridge* and what its equivalent is in their first language. Some languages have a similar word to the French word *pont* (for example *ponte* in Italian) while others are completely different (for example *hid* in Hungarian). Afterwards, students match the ten equivalents for the word *bridge* in the ten languages given.
ANSWERS: 1d, 2g, 3a, 4f, 5h, 6b, 7e, 8c, 9j, 10i

3 Pairs
Students discuss questions a–c with a partner. If you think they may need help, you could provide some pictures to prompt them. Alternatively, move straight on to Activity A4.

4/5/6 Pairs
Students will get the answers to these three activities in the listening section of this unit. In Activity A4, they need to look at the pictures of six bridges and guess where they are. One or two may be recognisable (for example, 5 is Tower Bridge in London), but it is not important if students are unsure, so do not let them spend too much time speculating. In Activity A5, students match the bridges with the lengths. They probably won't have much of an idea, but let them guess. Finally, in Activity A6, they guess in which year the bridges were first opened.
ANSWERS:
1 Mahatma Gandhi Setu Bridge (India), 5850 m, 1982
2 Akashi-Kaikyo Bridge (Japan), 3911 m, 1998
3 Golden Gate Bridge (USA), 2700 m, 1937
4 Rio Antirio Bridge (Greece), 2880 m, 2004
5 Tower Bridge (England), 244 m, 1894
6 Tsing Ma Bridge (Hong Kong), 1377 m, 1997

B Listening (Coursebook page 122)

1/2 Whole class, then pairs
Prepare students for the audio by checking that they understand who they are going to listen to (Fadi, a student in Jeddah), what they are going to hear (a talk about the six bridges) and what they have to do while listening (decide which bridge Fadi is talking about). Before they listen, students work in pairs and match the phrases a–f to the six bridges they have already looked at. They can use paper or digital reference sources to help with any difficult vocabulary. Then they listen to Fadi and decide which of the six bridges in the list he is talking about.

TRACK 15

Hi, my name's Fadi and I'm going to tell you about the six bridges I researched for my school project.

Opened in 1998, at 3911 metres in length, this bridge is currently the world's largest three-span suspension bridge, linking Kobe to Awaji Island across the Akashi Strait. Previously, ferries operated across the water, until a fatal crash convinced the Japanese government to build a bridge which could also withstand winds of 286 kilometres per hour, sea currents and earthquakes.

This 2880-metre long bridge spans the Gulf of Corinth and was officially opened the day before the 2004 Athens Olympics started. The depth of water in the Gulf can reach 65 metres, so the bridge supports are not buried in the seabed, but rest on it. This means that the supports can move sideways in the event of an earthquake.

This bridge connects Patna, in the south, with Hajipur, in the north, and spans the Ganges River. It was opened in 1982 and, at 5850 metres, it is believed to be the world's longest single river bridge.

This is the world's longest rail and road suspension bridge, spanning 1377 metres. It was opened in 1997 and has two decks, for road and rail traffic: a dual three-lane carriageway on the upper deck, and a two-lane emergency roadway and two railway tracks below.

When it was opened in 1937, this was the world's longest suspension bridge. At 2700 metres, it is currently the second longest suspension bridge, after New York City's Verrazano-Narrows Bridge.

This famous landmark was opened in June 1894 by the Prince of Wales (later Edward VII). It is 244 metres long and has two towers, each rising to a height of 65 metres above the River Thames. Originally, there were two high-level walkways for pedestrians between the towers, but these were closed in 1910.

ANSWERS:
(B1): **a** Tower Bridge, **b** Mahatma Gandhi Setu Bridge, **c** Golden Gate Bridge, **d** Rio Antirio Bridge, **e** Akashi-Kaikyo Bridge, **f** Tsing Ma Bridge
(B2): **1** Akashi-Kaikyo Bridge, **2** Rio Antirio Bridge, **3** Mahatma Gandhi Setu Bridge, **4** Tsing Ma Bridge, **5** Golden Gate Bridge, **6** Tower Bridge

3/4 Alone
Students listen again and answer the questions a–g, then check their answers with the audioscript.

ANSWERS:
a Tsing Ma Bridge and Golden Gate Bridge
b Akashi-Kaikyo Bridge, Tsing Ma Bridge and Golden Gate Bridge
c Tower Bridge
d Tsing Ma Bridge
e Tower Bridge
f Golden Gate Bridge
g Akashi-Kaikyo Bridge

5 Pairs
Students discuss in pairs the most surprising thing about the bridges.

C Use of English: Verbs ending in -en (Coursebook pages 122–3)

1/2 Whole class, then pairs
Go through the information about verbs ending in -en in the blue box, then put students in pairs for Activity C1, in which they need to write the adjectives and nouns for the verbs provided. Then they use the appropriate form of one of the words from Activity C1 to complete sentences a–e. In some cases there may be more than one possible answer.

ANSWERS:
(C1): **a** wide/width, **b** broad/breadth, **c** strong/strength, **d** weak/weakness, **e** thick/ thickness
(C2): **a** strengthened, **b** height, **c** depth, **d** weaknesses, length, **e** widened

D Reading (Coursebook pages 123–4)

1 Pairs
Students work together to discuss their ideas about the hotel made of ice in Sweden. They can refer to the pictures on pages 123 and 124.

2/3 Pairs
Students decide which pieces of information a–e they will read about in the text. In Activity D3, they create five questions using the phrases from the previous activity.

POSSIBLE ANSWERS:
a How old is the hotel? / What is the age of the hotel?
b What facilities does the hotel have/offer?
c Where is the hotel (located)?
d How big is the hotel? / What is the size of the hotel?
e Where does the ice come from? / Where do they get the ice from?

4/5 Alone
Working alone, students skim the text and check in which paragraphs the pieces of information listed in Activity D2 appear. They should then find the answers to the questions they wrote in Activity D3.

ANSWERS:
(D4): **a** paragraph 1, **b** 3/4, **c** 1/4, **d** 4, **e** 3
(D5): **a** now in its twentieth year, **b** bar, reception, art gallery, cinema, chapel/church, **c** Jukkasjärvi, in the heart of Swedish Lapland, **d** the world's largest igloo, **e** the Torne River

6 Alone, then pairs
Students need to look at the text again, this time in more detail, and write five questions of their own for their partner to answer.

E Use of English: Intensifying adjectives (Coursebook page 125)

1 Whole class, then alone
Go through the information about intensifying adjectives in the blue box. Then, in pairs, students refer back to the text about the Icehotel and find five more examples of word combinations that use intensifying adjectives.

ANSWERS: complete winter break, entire Icehotel, entire creation, utter chaos, total change, absolute harmony

2 Whole class, then alone, then pairs
Go through the gapped sentences a–g orally, getting ideas from students about how to complete each one.

57

Then students work alone, choosing an appropriate intensifying adjective for each sentence. There may be more than one possible answer. If time allows, get students to come up with their own sentences, including an intensifying adjective in each one.

POSSIBLE ANSWERS:

a utter/complete/total/absolute
b complete/total
c complete/total
d entire
e entire
f utter/complete/total/absolute
g utter/total/complete/absolute

F Reading and writing
(Coursebook pages 125–7)

1/2 Whole class, then pairs
Introduce the topic of Atlantis and find out what students know about the 'lost city'. If they do not know very much, move on to Activity F2 and get students to guess if statements a–e are true or false. They will find out the answers later in this section.

3 Alone, then groups of four
Allocate one of the four texts – A, B, C or D – to students in groups of four. It is important that they only look at their own text, not the other three. They need to read their text, then look at the questions a–l and identify **three** questions that relate to the text they have just read. The other nine questions relate to the other texts.

After answering the three questions relating to their own text, students should find the answers to the other nine questions by asking the other three members of their group. At the end of the activity, students should have found the answers to all 12 questions.

ANSWERS:

a paragraph A – 9000 years ago
b C – scientists
c D – nobody
d D – made fun of him
e C – Gibraltar, south-west England, Bolivia, Caribbean, Azores, Canary Islands, Iceland, Sweden, western Africa, Sahara Desert
f D – didn't believe it
g B – based on fact, not myth
h B – earthquake
i B – sank an island
j A – 360 BCE
k C – nobody knows
l A – Europe and Africa

DIFFERENTIATED ACTIVITY

For weaker students, tell them which questions relate to which text.

For stronger students, put them into pairs rather than groups of four, and allocate two texts to each student.

4/5 Alone, then small groups
Using their answers from Activity F3, students write two paragraphs about Atlantis. Each paragraph should be 30–40 words long. The first paragraph should include information about texts A and B and the second paragraph information about texts C and D. Students are not allowed to look back at the text and must only use the answers from Activity F3. When they have finished writing the two paragraphs, students form small groups with people who have read the other texts. Then they read each other's texts and compare the content with their paragraphs and decide whose version is closest to the original.

DIFFERENTIATED ACTIVITY

For weaker students, reduce the amount of writing by asking them to write about either paragraphs A and B **or** C and D (not both). Also, you could allow them a short amount of time to look back at the texts.

For stronger students, get them to write four paragraphs, one for each text A, B, C and D, about 30–40 words each. They can only use their written answers from Activity F3, plus anything they can remember from the texts, so they will need to use more complex sentences to increase the words in each paragraph.

G Project work (Coursebook page 127)
Students complete a copy of the table with information they have researched. Then they choose one of the buildings or structures and create an information leaflet about it, which should include pictures and other visuals.

Coursebook materials

UNIT 16: Where are the Seven Wonders of the Ancient World?

Unit introduction

In this unit, the topics are **wonders of the world, modern and futuristic structures** and **Mumbai**, and the Use of English areas are *is thought/said/believed,* etc. and **compound nouns and complex noun phrases**.

A Speaking and thinking
(Coursebook pages 128–9)

1/2 Whole class, then pairs
Introduce the topic, then put students in pairs to talk about the Seven Wonders of the Ancient World. If students don't know much about the Wonders, get them to look at the pictures as this may give them some ideas. However, it is not important at this stage to know too much about them – even their names. The pictures show 1 the Temple of Artemis, 2 the Great Pyramid of Giza, 3 the Lighthouse of Alexandria, 4 the Mausoleum at Halicarnassus, 5 the Hanging Gardens of Babylon. The two missing are the Statue of Zeus and the Colossus of Rhodes.

3 Pairs
Students' geography skills will be useful for this activity. They need to decide which of the Seven Wonders is located in each place (A–G) on the map. Point out that three countries (Egypt, Greece and Turkey) each have two Wonders. Get students to think about why the Seven Wonders were built in these locations (Eastern Mediterranean and Near East).

ANSWERS: A = the Statue of Zeus, B = the Colossus of Rhodes, C = the Temple of Artemis, D = the Mausoleum at Halicarnassus, E = the Lighthouse of Alexandria, F = the Great Pyramid of Giza, G = the Hanging Gardens of Babylon

4 Pairs
The Seven Wonders of the Ancient World were built between about 2582 and 280 BCE, and today only one survives (the Great Pyramid of Giza). Students look at the timeline and guess when each Wonder was constructed. At this point you should provide the names of the structures, as students will need to write these on a copy of the timeline. Note that the dates given are estimates only, and different experts offer slightly different dates for the construction of the Seven Wonders.

ANSWERS: see table below

5 Pairs, then whole class
For this activity, students think about any other ancient structures they are familiar with, either in their own country or somewhere else, and make a list. Do some class feedback so that everyone can hear the ideas.

B Reading (Coursebook pages 130–1)

1 Pairs
Students are going to read a text about the Seven Wonders of the Ancient World, but before they do so they need to check on the meaning of the 11 words in the box. They can use paper or digital reference sources for help.

2 Alone, then pairs
Tell students to quickly read the text and decide which of the Seven Wonders each paragraph is referring to. Then they can compare answers with a partner.

ANSWERS: 1 = Great Pyramid of Giza, 2 = Hanging Gardens of Babylon, 3 = Temple of Artemis, 4 = Statue of Zeus, 5 = Mausoleum at Halicarnassus, 6 = Colossus of Rhodes, 7 = Lighthouse of Alexandria

Great Pyramid	Hanging Gardens of Babylon	Temple of Artemis	Statue of Zeus	Mausoleum At Halicarnassus	Colossus of Rhodes	Lighthouse of Alexandria
2584 BCE (= about 4600 years ago)	600 (= about 2615 years ago)	550 (= about 2565 years ago)	435 (= about 2450 years ago)	351 (= about 2365 years ago)	292 (= about 2300 years ago)	280 (= about 2295 years ago)

3 Alone, then pairs

Students now read the text in more detail and fill in the gaps a–k with the words from Activity B1.

ANSWERS: a tomb, **b** constructed, **c** borders, **d** lush, **e** irrigation, **f** controversy, **g** fame, **h** erected, **i** throne, **j** disassembled, **k** entire

4 Alone, then pairs

Before students write the answers to the questions, remind them to look for the key word/s and to think about the type of answer each question requires.

ANSWERS:

a four (the Hanging Gardens of Babylon, the Mausoleum at Halicarnassus, the Colossus of Rhodes and the Lighthouse of Alexandria)

b one (the Great Pyramid of Giza)

c the Hanging Gardens of Babylon

d the Colossus of Rhodes

e the Statue of Zeus and the Colossus of Rhodes

f Herostratus (the Temple of Artemis)

g the Great Pyramid of Giza and the Mausoleum at Halicarnassus

C Use of English: *is thought/ said/believed*, etc.

(Coursebook page 131)

1 Whole class, then alone

Go through the information about *is thought/said/ believed*, etc. in the blue box, then get students to use the words and phrases a–e in Activity C1 to write complete sentences. You could get oral feedback from the class before they write their answers.

ANSWERS (Box): *was thought to have been built, is said to have been destroyed*

ANSWERS (C1):

a The Colosseum is believed to have been built in the years 70–82.

b The Great Wall of China is thought to have been constructed about 2200 years ago.

c The Great Wall of China is said to have been guarded by more than 1 million soldiers.

d Machu Picchu is thought to have been deserted by the Incas because of disease.

e 'El Castilla' in the middle of Chich'en Itza is considered to have been a temple.

2 Alone, then pairs

Make sure that students understand what they have to do and go over the example with them. Students work alone and write five of their own *people say* sentences, then rewrite them using the passive

structure *is thought/said/believed*, etc. When they have finished, students compare their answers with a partner.

D Listening and writing

(Coursebook 131–2)

1 Whole class, then pairs

Prepare students for the audio by checking that they understand what they are going to listen to (an interview), what they are going to hear (information about New7Wonders) and what they have to do while listening (check answers to prediction questions). Before they listen, students work in pairs to decide which of the three options is most likely to be the main aim of the organisation New7Wonders.

2/3 Pairs

Working in pairs, students firstly need to check the meanings of the eight phrases in the box, and decide which they think they hear in the interview. They can use paper or digital reference sources for help. Then, students unjumble the letters of the nine different countries in Activity D3.

ANSWERS: Peru, Italy, Mexico, England, India, China, Brazil, Jordan, Switzerland

4 Alone

Now students listen and check their answers for the two previous activities, as well as for the main aim of the organisation New7Wonders (*to protect our heritage and history*).

TRACK 17

Renanda Sosa: I'm very pleased to welcome Carlos Gimenez to our programme. Today he's going to be talking to me about the 'seven wonders of the world'. Carlos, we've all heard about the Seven Wonders of the Ancient World, but what is all this about the new seven wonders of the world?

Carlos Gimenez: Well, Renanda, back in 2001, a gentleman from Switzerland by the name of Bernard Weber set up an organisation called New7Wonders. The purpose of New7Wonders is to protect our heritage and our history.

RS: How?

CG: By raising public awareness through the Internet, TV, the radio, and books and magazines.

RS: Is this global, or only in one particular country or continent?

CG: Oh, it's definitely worldwide, and anyone can join the organisation in order to help.

RS: What has New7Wonders done to protect the world's heritage and history?

CG: Well, one of the most interesting things it has done was to organise a vote by the general public for the new seven wonders of the world.

RS: How was this done?

CG: It was an online poll in 2007. The only criterion was that people had to choose a structure that had been built before 2000.

RS: I see. And what were the results? Were there any surprises?

CG: To be honest, the results were rather predictable and include structures which are said to be very popular with tourists, as well as historians.

RS: For example?

CG: Well, the Colosseum in Rome, Italy, the Great Wall of China and the Taj Mahal in India are all in the seven.

RS: Let me guess … what about Petra in Jordan? Was that voted for?

CG: Yes, Petra is there, along with Machu Picchu in Peru, and the wonderful statue of Christ the Redeemer in Rio, Brazil.

RS: Hmm, that makes six, I think. What's the final one? Stonehenge?

CG: No, not Stonehenge in England. It's Chich'en Itza, probably the least well known of the seven new wonders.

RS: Where is it, exactly?

CG: Chich'en Itza is a Mayan city in Mexico, and is a wonderful architectural site.

RS: What will the outcome be of this poll? Will these seven structures now be protected for ever?

CG: Unfortunately, publicity is not always a good thing. One major concern is that tourists will now flock to these places and put an added strain on them. It is believed they could ultimately be destroyed, rather than be protected.

RS: That really is a sad reality, isn't it?

5   **Whole class, then alone, then pairs**
Go through the notes that students need to complete when they listen for a second time. Ask them to predict their answers orally, then play the audio

again. As they listen, students write their answers for the gaps a–h (as well as checking their predictions).
ANSWERS: a 2001, **b** history, **c** public awareness, **d** online poll/vote, **e** structures, **f** Mexico, **g** Brazil, **h** a strain on

6   **Pairs, then alone**
Students work together and talk about the new seven wonders of the world and whether or not they agree with the selection. They should also think of a structure that they believe deserves to be on the list. Then, students write an email to a local online newspaper, in which they try to persuade the readers about their choice. They need to describe the structure and its location, and say why they think it should be included in the list.

E Use of English: Compound nouns and complex noun phrases (Coursebook pages 132–3)

1   **Whole class, then alone, then pairs**
Go through the information about compound nouns and complex noun phrases in the blue box, then put students into pairs and ask them refer back to the email they wrote in Activity D6. They need to identify any subjects or objects that are single pronouns and decide if they could be made more interesting or specific by using a compound noun or complex noun phrase. Give students some time to do this, after which they can show their partner any changes they have made.

F Reading (Coursebook pages 133–5)

1   **Pairs**
Introduce the topic, then allow students a couple of minutes to discuss what they know about Mumbai. They should write down three things, if possible. If students are totally unfamiliar with the city, get them to write down three things that they would like to know, for example *What is the population of Mumbai?* If students are actually based in Mumbai, or in India, and are already knowledgeable about the city, tell them to write down what they think are the three most interesting things about the city.

2   **Alone, then groups of four**
In this activity, students are going to work alone at first and then in small groups to check the meanings of the words and phrases. They can use paper or digital reference sources for help, and make notes in a copy of the table. When everyone has checked the

61

meaning of their five words and phrases, students join up to make A/B/C/D groups to talk about their answers.

For weaker students, put them into groups (A or B or C or D) so that they can help each other to find the meanings of the words and phrases.

For stronger students, allocate them two groups of words and phrases (A and B or C and D).

3   Alone, then pairs

Now students skim the text and check if the meanings they found in the previous activity were correct.

4   Alone, then pairs

Before students answer the questions, remind them to identify the key word/s in each question and to think about the type of answer each question requires. Then students write their answers and compare them with a partner.

ANSWERS:

a   Bollywood films, bumper-to-bumper traffic
b   vibrant, colourful, compact, walkable
c   (masala) tea, fresh milk, fish
d   because there is shopping for every budget, style and taste
e   they don't tend to open until about 11 a.m., and some of them can be hard to find
f   Regal Cinema
g   colossal staircase and photographic display
h   around the corner from the Taj
i   various possible answers, but they should agree that the writer feels 'positive'

G Project work (Coursebook page 135)

Students are going to read about three modern, futuristic structures, then choose one as the basis for a poster presentation. They will need to research their chosen structure and use the information they collect in their class presentation.

Coursebook materials

UNIT 17: What impact does fashion have on teenagers?

Unit introduction

In this unit, the topics are **technology** and **design and fashion**, and the Use of English areas are **word building** and **modal verbs**.

A Speaking and thinking
(Coursebook page 136)

1/2 Whole class, then pairs
Introduce the topic, then put students in pairs to discuss and complete Activities A1 and A2. Note that for question A1d students are asked to design a graph or chart that displays the results of their discussions about free-time activities. They can either do this alone or with a partner.

3/4 Alone, then pairs
Get students to think about how their parents and grandparents might have entertained themselves when they were teenagers, and if these ways would have been different from the ways in which young people entertain themselves today. Working alone, get students to make a list, then compare their list with their partner's. In Activity A4 they continue the discussion, this time thinking about the future and how the things we do in our free time might change.

B Reading and vocabulary
(Coursebook pages 136–8)

1 Whole class, then pairs
Ask students what the word *digital* means and if they can think of any items that contain the word *digital* – for example *digital clock*. Then get them to focus on the short definition and complete gaps a–i using the words in the box. They can check with a partner when they have finished.
ANSWERS: a digits, **b** computer, **c** information, **d** movies, **e** digitised, **f** black or white, **g** dots, **h** continuous, **i** transmit

2 Pairs
Many students will own their own mobile (cell) phone, or know someone who has one. For this activity they need to think of things that a mobile phone can do, and what people actually use their phones for.

3 Pairs
Students look at the information in the table, which shows some statistics about how teenagers use their mobile phones. They need to match the statistics in the left-hand column with the facts in the right-hand column, then check to see if their partner agrees. Do the statistics surprise them?
ANSWERS:
83% = use phones to take pictures
60% = play music on phones
46% = play games on their phones
31% = exchange instant messages on their phones
23% = access social networks on their phones
21% = use email on their phones

4/5 Pairs
All the phrases in the box appear in the text about mobile phones that students are going to read. First they need to use paper or digital reference sources to check the meanings of the phrases in the box, then they should skim the text to find the phrases and to check that they have understood them correctly.

6 Alone, then pairs
Go through questions a–e, making sure that students understand what they need to look for in each paragraph. They should work on their own to find the answers before checking them with a partner.
ANSWERS:
a (i) teenagers, adolescent, (ii) an expression of identity
b (i) absolutely critical, (ii) rarely
c (i) entertainment, (ii) various answers possible, (iii) various answers possible
d (i) ease, accessibility, (ii) generation
e (i) having a healthy social life, (ii) portable digital entertainment units, (iii) they can occupy their minds and hands, (iv) to be redirected to new destinations within seconds, (v) ability to let your parents know where you are

C Use of English: Word building
(Coursebook pages 138–9)

1 Alone
Students make a copy of the table and then work on their own to fill in as many gaps as they can. For each of the eight adjectives listed, students should also think of an equivalent descriptive word in their own language.

ANSWERS:

Adjective	Noun	Verb	Adverb
essential	essence		essentially
healthy	health		healthily
social	society	socialise	socially
critical	critic	criticise	critically
immediate	immediacy		immediately
previous			previously
mobile	mobile, mobility	mobilise	

2 Alone, then pairs
Still working on their own, students fill in the gaps in sentences a–e with suitable words from the previous activity. When they have written something in all the gaps, they can compare their answers with a partner.

ANSWERS: a social, **b** essential, **c** immediately, **d** society, **e** criticise

3 Alone
For further practice using the words from Activity C1, students choose three words that they did not use in Activity C2 and use them in three sentences of their own. Each sentence should say something about teenagers and their mobile phones.

D Reading and speaking
(Coursebook pages 139–40)

1/2 Pairs, then whole class
In pairs, students discuss questions a–c, then consider how fashion will be different in the future: ten years from now and 20 years from now. When they have had time to answer the questions, each pair can share their ideas with the class.

3 Pairs
Working in pairs students firstly need to check the meanings of *prototypes* and *biometric bodysuits*. Tell students to look at the prefixes *proto-* and *bio-* as

a way of helping them to understand what the words mean. They can also use paper or digital reference sources for help. If possible, they should also find equivalent words in their own language.

4 Alone, then pairs
Deal with any difficult vocabulary, then get students to predict what they think a biometric bodysuit will be able to do.

5 Alone
Students skim the text on the following page to check if the points mentioned in Activity D4 are covered in the information (they are all mentioned).

6 Alone, then pairs
Students work alone to find the words or phrases in the text that have similar meanings to the words and phrases given. Because there is a large number to find, you could divide up a–n between different groups of students.

ANSWERS: a detect, **b** version, **c** lightweight, **d** monitor, **e** wearable, **f** incorporated, **g** aesthetic, **h** civilian, **i** embedded, **j** promote, **k** diagnose, **l** blending, **m** fabric, **n** generate

DIFFERENTIATED ACTIVITY

For weaker students, reduce the number of words and phrases they need to find, and/or supply the words and phrases from the text so students can match them to the meanings a–n. Another possibility is to provide options for each word or phrase, and get students to choose the best one. You could also allow them to work in small groups, thus providing support for one another.

For stronger students, you could provide them with the same list of words and phrases as in the Coursebook, but without the paragraph numbers to help them.

7 Alone, then pairs
Before students write the answers to questions a–e, remind them to look for the key word/s in each question, and to think about the type of answer each question requires. Then students write their answers and compare them with a partner.

ANSWERS:

a with a rise in body temperature
b military version uses fuel cells
c functional – source of power, aesthetic – change appearance
d shows where electronic and fluid devices are
e using the technology in building design

8 Pairs, then whole class

Students discuss what other things they would like the bodysuit to do, drawing up a list as they talk. Then they share their ideas with other students to find out if they are the same or different.

E Use of English: Modal verbs
(Coursebook page 141)

1 Whole class, then alone, then pairs

Go through the information about modal verbs in the blue box, then on their own students refer back to the *Biometric bodysuits* text to find ten more examples of a modal verb + a main verb. When they have found all ten, they can compare their lists in pairs.

ANSWERS: *can monitor, will even be able, should reach, could give, might be incorporated, could be embedded, could diagnose, could all be made, could produce, would help*

2 Alone, then pairs

Students make a copy of the table and then add the modal verbs from Activity E1, plus any others they know for showing possibility and ability.

ANSWERS:

Possibility	Ability
should, could, might, would may, must	can, will be able could, will be able to, could have

3 Pairs

Students look at the modal verbs in Activity E2 and decide what other functions they have. For example in the text, *can* is used for ability, but it *can* also be used for asking for permission: *Can I borrow your new jacket?*

Permission: *could, might, would, may, can*

Advice: *should, could*

When students have made a list of modals with their various functions, they should write eight sentences, using a different modal verb in each one.

F Listening and writing
(Coursebook pages 141–2)

1/2 Whole class, then pairs

Check that students understand who they are going to listen to (a historian) and what the person is going to talk about (the clothes people used to wear in the past), as well as what they have to do when they listen (check their answers). Before they listen,

students work in pairs and decide if statements a–f are true or false, giving their reasons. Then they listen and check their answers (all the statements are true).

TRACK 18

Welcome, everyone, to this month's history programme. My name is Abir al Hadi and today I'm going to be talking to you about clothes!

Clothing was very expensive in the ancient and medieval world because, without engine-powered machines, it was very hard to make. So most people had very few changes of clothing; many people probably owned only the clothes they were wearing. Many children had no clothes at all and just went naked.

In the Stone Age, most clothing was made of leather or fur, or woven grasses. By the Bronze Age, people had learned to spin yarn on a spindle and to weave cloth out of the yarn on looms. Although many clothes, especially coats, were still made out of leather or fur, most clothes were made out of wool (from sheep), linen (from the flax plant) or cotton. Some rich people wore silk. In the Middle Ages, people invented the spinning wheel, which made spinning yarn about four times faster. Clothes were a little less expensive than they had been before, but still most people had only one or two outfits.

People wore different kinds of clothes. Clothes helped to show where you were from, and whether you were rich or poor, and whether you were a girl or a boy.

Around the Mediterranean – in Egypt, North Africa, Greece and the Roman Empire – people mostly wore wool or linen tunics (like a big T-shirt). Women wore long tunics and men mostly wore short ones. Over their tunic, they might wear a wool cloak, if it was cold. Further north, in Europe, a lot of men wore wool trousers under their tunics, as you probably do today.

In west Asia, both tunics and trousers were also pretty common, but they were made out of linen, and then in the Islamic period people began to use more silk and cotton.

In China too, people wore tunics, and a lot of people wore trousers. Their tunics and trousers were made out of hemp, ramie and silk, and later out of cotton.

But in India and Africa, people mainly made their clothes without sewing, out of one big piece of cloth wrapped around themselves in various ways, like a woman's sari in India, or her kanga in central Africa. Most people's clothes were made out of cotton or silk.

Adapted from www.historyforkids.org

3   Alone, then pairs

Students make a copy of the table, then listen again and complete the notes. When they have finished, they compare their notes with their partner's.

ANSWERS:

	Information about clothes
Stone Age	made of leather or fur, or woven grasses
Bronze Age	many clothes, especially coats, still made of leather or fur, most clothes made of wool, linen or cotton; rich people wore silk
Middle Ages	clothes less expensive, but people still only had one or two outfits
Mediterranean region	people wore wool or linen tunics – women long, men short; wool cloaks
West Asia	tunics and trousers common, made of linen
China	tunics, and many people wore trousers; hemp, ramie, silk, cotton
India and Africa	clothes without sewing, one big piece of cloth wrapped around the body, e.g. sari in India, kanga in central Africa; made of cotton or silk

4   Alone

Now students write an article for their school's web page, using information from the talk as well as their notes from Activity F3. The article should focus on the clothes people wore in the past.

5   Alone, then pairs

This is a mini-research activity. First students work alone and select three countries from the listening text. They should find out in what ways clothing today is different from clothing in the past. They then add a third column to the table and include information about clothes today. When they have completed the table they can share their ideas with a partner.

G Project work (Coursebook page 142)

For this project, students can choose how to present their research to the class. They need to design their own biometric bodysuit, using ideas from the Internet, but also their own imagination and creativity. The presentation should include pictures and other visuals, along with any information they have found.

Coursebook materials
UNIT 18: What does that sign mean?

Unit introduction

In this unit, the topics are **symbols**, **superheroes** and **sign language**, and the Use of English areas are **position of adjectives** and **semi-fixed and fixed expressions**.

A Speaking and thinking
(Coursebook page 143)

1 **Whole class, then pairs**
Signs and symbols are all around us – and many have an international meaning. Students look at Activity A1 and say what the signs and symbols mean.

ANSWERS:
1 = no smoking
2 = the sign used for email addresses
3 = smiley face showing happiness
4 = 'I am greater than you' (the '>' sign means 'greater than')
5 = technology is available to assist those with hearing difficulties (in a shop or bank, for example)
6 = female/male signs commonly seen in Middle Eastern countries

2 **Pairs**
Students think about the purpose of signs and symbols, whether they instruct or order us to do something or if they merely give us information. Get students to look back at the signs and symbols in Activity A1 and decide if they instruct, order or inform. Do any serve more than one purpose?

3 **Whole class**
Classrooms and school corridors are usually full of signs and symbols, giving instructions (for example in case of an emergency), informing students about something (examination dates) or ordering (for example not to run in the corridor). Get students to look around the classroom (and outside if possible) to see what signs and symbols are on display and to say what they mean. If there are no signs or symbols nearby, get students to make some up (or move on to Activity A4).

4 **Pairs**
For this activity, students need to think of a public place, such as an airport, a hospital, or a shopping centre (not their school), and discuss which of the signs and symbols from Activity A1 they might see there. If possible, get each pair to choose a different location. In 4b, students think about what other signs and symbols they might see, as each location would need to inform/order/instruct people about different things.

5 **Whole class**
Go through the information in Activity A5, pointing out to students that there is no name for the @ symbol in English, even though other languages have one. What is it called in their own language? Some other names for this symbol mean *monkey*, *cabbage*, *twiddle*, *twist*, *a-twist*, *whirlpool*, *cyclone*, *ape*, *cat*, *rose*.

6 **Alone, then pairs**
In the text there are two theories for the origin of the @ symbol. Students read the text alone and decide which theory they prefer, then discuss with a partner. Find out from the whole class which is the most popular theory.

B Reading (Coursebook pages 144–5)

1 **Whole class**
Focus on the symbol and find out what students think it means. If you can do this by showing a picture of the symbol on the board, students will not be able to look ahead to the text and find the answer there!

2 **Pairs**
Before students read the text about the international peace symbol, they should work together to find out the meanings of the words and phrases in the box.

3/4 **Alone, then pairs**
Students skim the text and check if their ideas from Activity B1 were correct. They should then read the text more closely, filling the gaps with the words from Activity B2.

ANSWERS: a nuclear disarmament, **b** despair, **c** palm, **d** in the manner of, **e** quickly spread, **f** emblem, **g** campaign, **h** migrated, **i** copyrighted

5 Alone, then pairs

Before students write answers to questions a–e, remind them to identify the key word/s and to think about the type of answer each question requires. When they have finished, students can compare their answers with a partner.

ANSWERS:
a a symbol for the DAC
b semaphore letters
c in the painting the arms go up
d so that it is free for everyone to use
e despair about nuclear war

C Use of English: Position of adjectives (Coursebook page 145)

1 Whole class, then alone

Go through the information about the position of adjectives in the blue box, then get students to rewrite sentences a–e using a different adjective (but with a similar meaning) in each one.

ANSWERS: a older, **b** alive, **c** frightened, **d** afloat, **e** asleep

DIFFERENTIATED ACTIVITY

For weaker students, provide them with the missing words (*older, alive, frightened, afloat, asleep*) and also five distractors (which do not all have to be adjectives), for example *eldest, living, scary, float, sleep*.

For stronger students, get them to rewrite the sentences without the help of the gapped sentences in the Coursebook.

2 Alone, then pairs

Working on their own, students rewrite sentences a–c, in each case changing the position of the adjective. Do this orally first. When students have rewritten the sentences they can check with their partner.

ANSWERS:
a The position of the two semaphore letters is *simplified*.
b *The symbol was new and quickly spread.*
c *Everybody can have the symbol for free.*

3 Alone, then pairs

Students need to go back to the text and find some examples of adjectives + nouns. They should then rewrite these with the adjective in the predicative position.

ANSWERS:
These long boring copying duties were performed by monks.
Grain, spices and liquids were transported in large terracotta jars.

D Listening (Coursebook pages 146–7)

1/2 Whole class, then pairs

Discuss the questions about superheroes with the class, using pictures of superheroes as prompts if you think it necessary. For Activity D2, students work in pairs to talk about what superheroes do and what qualities they need to have.

3/4 Alone, then pairs

Students read the text quickly to check if their ideas from Activity D2 are the same as the ideas in the text. Then they make a list of the qualities the text says a superhero needs to have and compare their list with a partner.

ANSWERS: brave, protect others, have courage, have self-discipline, help others solve their problems, extraordinary physical strength and skills, amazing mental abilities, never give up

5 Pairs

Check that students understand who they are going to listen to (a superhero fanatic) and what the person is going to talk about (the history of superheroes and their symbols), as well as what they have to do when they listen (check their answers). Before they listen, students work in pairs and decide if each of the five pieces of information given is true or false, giving their reasons. Then students use paper or digital reference sources to check the meanings of the words and phrases in the box.

6 Alone, then pairs

Students listen and check their answers to Activity D5.

TRACK 19

Interviewer: Welcome to this week's edition of 'Entertainment Plus'! Today I'm talking to Hilary Manor, a superhero fanatic! Hi, Hilary!

Hilary Manor: Hello, Jason, thanks for inviting me.

Int: It's good to have you here, Hilary, to tell us something about the history of superheroes.

HM: Well, to be honest, it's hard to think about the history of superheroes without considering Superman and Batman and their famous, iconic symbols. Superheroes became popular in the late 1930s and early 1940s, and during World War II, they became international stars. Since then, numerous books, television shows and movies have been published and produced about superheroes, and they are known throughout the world, some of them perhaps even more than real historic figures.

Int: Isn't it true that Superman and Batman first appeared in comics?

HM: You're absolutely right! The first Action Comics was published in 1938, and it featured a man with a red cape and blue costume who was strong enough to lift an automobile over his head. Do you know who that was?

Int: Superman, of course!

HM: Yes, Superman had arrived and he became the first comic-book character to have powers much greater than any human being. The stage was set for other fantastic characters to follow.

Int: So who was next? Spider-Man?

HM: I'm afraid not. Next in line, in 1941, was the first female superhero.

Int: The woman with the double W symbol? Wonder Woman?

HM: Spot on! She may have begun life as a secretary, but Wonder Woman became as popular as Superman and Batman. Glamorous, strong and intelligent, she acquired incredible powers, and she has bullet-proof wrist bands and a magic, golden lasso! Her double W symbol is just as famous as Superman's and Batman's.

Int: Didn't some of the superheroes start to lose popularity?

HM: Temporarily, yes. In the 1950s, many superhero characters lost their popularity. There were many other comic books being published and these publications had to compete against the new arrival called television. The superhero age almost ended. But comic-book-publishing companies relaunched some characters and the superheroes have been successful ever since.

Int: Thank goodness! So where are we now? The 1960s?

HM: Yes. By 1964, sales of the Batman comic books had fallen significantly and the publishers were thinking about killing him off.

Int: Are you serious?

HM: Absolutely! But once again a superhero was saved. When Batman came to television in 1966, his popularity soared to new heights. In 1966, the Batman movie brought further interest, as did the cartoon series.

Int: Now here's something. I've noticed nowadays the character of some superheroes is changing. They make mistakes, and they seem to have some human qualities. Am I right?

HM: Yes, you are. In the 1970s and 1980s, comic-book superheroes began to show some human faults and to have personal problems. But this makes them more interesting, I think.

Int: I totally agree, Hilary. So where are our superheroes today? Can we expect to keep on seeing those iconic symbols everywhere?

HM: That's an absolute certainty! Today, superheroes continue to be more popular than ever. Movies that star characters such as Spider-Man have become blockbusters. *Avengers Assemble*, which was released in 2012, is one of the most financially successful movies of all time! And, because of their renewed popularity, the demand for T-shirts, posters, calendars, and so on, all printed with those amazing symbols, has increased beyond imagination. The superheroes, many now in graphic novels, as well as comic books, are much more sophisticated, with multiple sides to their personalities, but their power lives on.

Int: Thanks, Hilary, for a really interesting mini-history of the superheroes!

Adapted from www.mania.com

ANSWERS: all are true

7/8 Alone, then whole class, then pairs
Students make their own copy of the table. When they are ready, go through each gap a–l, asking students what type of information they need to use to complete the gaps, and pointing out that they will need to write more than one word for most answers. Students listen and complete the notes, then check with their partner. They can also look at the audioscript on page 158 if they are not sure about something.

ANSWERS:
a became popular
b international stars
c Action Comics
d Superman

e female superhero
f lost their popularity
g had fallen significantly
h Batman
i human faults
j personal problems
k popular
l sides to their

DIFFERENTIATED ACTIVITY

For weaker students, consider allowing them to read the audioscript **before** they do Activity D7, as this will help them to understand any points they are not sure about before they complete the notes.

For stronger students, you could supply them with a different version of the table, which contains less information (for example you could remove some of the dates in the left-hand column) and therefore increases how much they need to add. For example:

late 1930s and 1940s	superheroes (a) …
? …	became (b) …
1938	first (c) …, featured superhero called (d) …
? …	first (e) …
? …	many superheroes (f) …
by 1964	Batman comic book sales (g) …
in 1966	TV series and film for (h) …
? …	superheroes started to show (i) … and have (j) …
? …	superheroes more (k) … than ever, with more (l) … personalities

E Use of English: Semi-fixed and fixed expressions
(Coursebook pages 147–8)

1 **Whole class**
Go through the information about semi-fixed and fixed expressions in the blue box. This is quite a complex and controversial area, and different

people have different opinions not only about what semi-fixed and fixed expressions are, but also on the terminology used to describe them. Do not let students get bogged down with endless examples, but point out the difference between the two types of expression. Then refer students to the audioscript on page 158 to identify at least five more examples. You could do a couple as examples, as there are plenty for students to find in the audioscript.

ANSWERS: So who was next?, I'm afraid not, Spot on!, Temporarily, yes, Thank goodness!, Are you serious?, Now here's something, Am I right?, I totally agree, That's an absolute certainty!

F Reading and writing
(Coursebook pages 148–9)

1 **Pairs**
For this activity, make sure students do **not** look at the text while they are answering the questions. You could put the questions on the board or provide them on a handout so students work with their books closed.

2 **Alone**
Students read the text and check their guesses in Activity F1.
ANSWERS:
a hands and face
b no, there are different versions
c more than 200 years ago
d sight/vision
e raising their eyebrows
f yes

3 **Alone or small groups**
Depending on how you want to set this up, students could either prepare their speech alone or in small groups. Perhaps for weaker students, working with others will give them more confidence. Allow sufficient time to make notes from the text *What is sign language?*, and make sure they include information on what sign language is, its history, and the similarities and differences between spoken language and sign language. When they have completed their notes, students can write their speech. If you wish, you could get students to deliver their speeches orally as well, but the focus for this activity is on **writing** the speech.

DIFFERENTIATED ACTIVITY

For weaker students, if you decide that they are going to prepare the speech in small groups, allocate only one of the three areas (1 *what sign language is,* 2 *its history,* 3 *the similarities and differences between spoken language and sign language*) to each student. You can also specify that students need to find two or three pieces of information for each section. Then when they come to write the speech, each student focuses on just one area.

For stronger students, specify how many pieces of information for each section you want them to include in their speech. For example for Sections 1 and 2, this could be four pieces of information, whereas for Section 3, you could ask for more (as there is much more information in the text about the similarities and differences between spoken language and written language).

G Project work (Coursebook page 149)

For this project, students are going to research different methods of sending information without using modern-day technology. They need to copy the table and then research four methods of communication: Morse code, ship flags, fire beacons and smoke. Then students choose one method to present to the class, using any medium that they want (for example PowerPoint, information leaflet – or any other method from the Coursebook).

71

Workbook answers

UNIT 1: How many planets are there in space?

A1

Name of the planet in English	Name of god/goddess, if represented	Name of the planet in your language	Distance of the planet from the sun
Mercury	winged messenger	Various answers	58 million km
Venus	love and beauty	"	108 million km
Earth	none	"	150 million km
Mars	blood, war	"	228 million km
Jupiter	king	"	779 million km
Saturn	agriculture	"	1.43 billion km
Uranus	sky	"	2.88 billion km
Neptune	sea	"	4.50 billion km
Pluto	underworld	"	5.91 billion km

A2

Launch – send something off into the air
Mythical – imaginary, or not real
Parachute – a cloth canopy that allows something to descend slowly
Planet – a large round mass that orbits a star
Classified – arranged in a group according to features
Solar system – the sun, planets and moons
Desert – an empty, waterless area of land
Dwarf – something very small
Telescope – an instrument designed to make distant objects seem closer
Agriculture –the practice of farming
Volcano – a mountain with an opening from which lava comes
Lens – a piece of curved transparent material to send out light rays

B1

a and b contain passive verbs:
(a) are named,
(b) were given

B2

are produced / were given / have been sent / had been trained / will be required

B3

(a) are produced,
(b) is hit,
(c) are bent,
(d) is formed,
(e) is changed

B4

group / beginning / meaning

B5

a dis-, b tele-, c under-, d kilo-, e trans-, f un-, g de-

B6

a astro- = to do with the stars, b cosmo- = to do with the universe, c tele- = to do with distance, d agri- = to do with soil or field, e un- = meaning 'not' or the opposite

B7

a across [examples: transatlantic, transmission], b small [microscopic, microcosm], c above, beyond [supermarket, superimpose], e skill, art [technology, technical]

B8

a What was the name of Gagarin's spacecraft?
b Which country did he come from?
c Where did he fly / orbit?
d Why is he famous?
e How did he land back on Earth?
f When did Gagarin become the first man in space?

B9 – various answers possible

a What did he do on 14 October 2012? / He made a giant leap from 38 kilometres above the Earth; What was his nickname? / 'Fearless Felix'
b Which country did he come from? / Austria
c Where did he jump from? / 38 kilometres above Earth
d Why is he now famous? / He made a new world record
e How did he land in the desert in the Mexico? / He used a parachute; How long did he fall for? / Three minutes and 43 seconds; How long in total did the jump last? / Eight minutes and eight seconds; How many people watched his jump? / Around 52 million; How fast did he travel? / More than 1357.6kph
f When did he make the jump? / On 14th October 2012

C1

(b) during the years 25-220 CE,
(c) At a later date,
(d) in the 17th century,
(e) thousands of years ago

C2 – various answers possible

Venus is the brightest object in the sky, apart from the Sun and Moon. It is sometimes called the 'Morning Star' when it appears in the east at dawn, or the 'Evening Star' when it appears in the west at dusk. Thousands of years ago, the evening star was called Hesperus and the morning star was called Phosphorous. Because of Venus' and the Earth's distance from the Sun, Venus is never visible more than three hours before dawn and three hours after dusk. The planet is difficult to study from Earth because it is covered in clouds, and most knowledge comes from space vehicles. The very powerful radar on the Magellan spacecraft found huge active volcanoes on Venus.

Workbook answers
UNIT 2: What's a living creature?

A1

spotted: saw, noticed; identified: recognised, understood; temporarily: briefly, momentarily; float: drift, fly; rare: uncommon, unusual; sightings: findings, detections; denied: refused, rejected; hover: hang, glide

A2

a hover, hang
b float, glide

B1

<u>apparently</u>, <u>carefully</u>, <u>increasingly</u>, <u>always</u>, <u>quickly</u>, <u>never</u>

B2 – some variations possible

a carefully / quickly,
b apparently / increasingly,
c apparently,
d never,
e quickly,
f always / never

B3 – most common/useful words

a healthily (adverb), healthy (adjective)
b fertile (adj), fertilise (verb)
c production, producer, product, productivity (all nouns), productive (adj)
d energy (n), energetically (adv), energetic (adj)
e reproduce (vb), reproduction (n), reproductive (adj)
f sensitively (adv), sensitise (vb)
g responsive (adj), responsively (adv), response (n)
h growth (n)

B4

a healthy, b response, c energetic, d productivity,
e fertile, f reproductive, g sensitively, h growth

B5

When	Contrast	In addition
finally, firstly, lastly, secondly	although, but, even though, however, on the other hand	also, and, furthermore, or, so

C1/2

The Jurupa oak tree.

C3

d paragraph 3, g paragraphs 4 and 5

C4

d, e, f, b, c, a

C5

a False – a crescent area of the Middle East was fertile
b False – much of the world was covered in glaciers
c False – scientists believe it is the oldest living thing
d False – it has repeatedly renewed itself
e False – re-sprouting from roots
f True
g False – appears to be the last living remnant

D1/2 – various answers possible

The elephants in Thailand used to work in forests with loggers, but this is now illegal. So today the elephants live in a sanctuary because they cannot go back to the wild, and they 'paint' pictures for tourists, who buy the paintings. This is not a real painting of course. The elephant's keeper secretly guides the animal by pulling its ear, and the elephant always produces the same picture. The painting is a trick, but it is a clever trick because the animal interprets the message from its ear in order to activate its trunk.

Workbook answers
UNIT 3: What's a hurricane?

A1

a hailstorm,
b avalanche,
c flood,
d tsunami,
e mudslide,
f drought,
g earthquake,
h tornado,
i hurricane,
j sandstorm

A2

a+f, b+j, c+c, d+a, e+ i, f+d, g+h, h+b, i+g, j+e

A3

	antonym	synonym
awesome	disappointing	impressive
freedom	conformity	liberty
destruction	build/ construction	ruin/collapse
active	passive/ sluggish/slow	lively
light	heavy	weightless
progress	retreat	development
last	perish	continue
calm	agitated	peaceful
wealth	poverty	riches/money
brave	cowardly	courageous
trust	distrust	believe

B1

a anger,
b confidence,
c courage,
d danger,
e enjoyment,
f freedom,
g knowledge

B2

a Take notice of warning signs if you are in an avalanche area
b Try to get to the side of an avalanche if you are caught in the path of it
c If you are hit by an avalanche, try to swim with it
d If a hurricane approaches, hide in the basement
e If you live on a boat, be careful of broken power cables

B3

a If you see an eruption, warn others
b If you see buildings shaking, move to an open area
c If you walk in an avalanche area, never travel alone
d If you can't avoid an avalanche, try to hold on to something solid
e If you live in a mobile home, move out if danger is approaching

C1 – various answers possible

Americas: USA, Brazil, Mexico, Colombia, Argentina, etc
Caribbean: Cuba, Haiti, Dominican Republic, Puerto Rica, Jamaica, etc

C2

Americas: Brazil, Guyana, Mexico, USA, Bahamas, Bermuda, Canada, Alaska, Chile, Peru
Caribbean: Trinidad and Tobago, Jamaica

C3

a for identification purposes, b since 1978, meteorologists choose them, c each year, d men's and women's names, e no, some are given letters from the Greek alphabet

C4

a True, b True, c True, d False – public awareness grew, not interest, e True, f True g True, h True

D1

a The floods are some of the worst seen since 2011.
b Yes, for another week.

D2

a 4
b 2
c 3
d 1
e 3

D3

a a week
b displaced
c forecasts
d reservoirs
e drove

D4

Water in Sri Lanka

Charities give equipment for cleaning dirty water, which removes bacteria but not salt. Charities also give people tanks for collecting monsoon rain water. There is a project to dig more wells for water and already some are providing clean drinking water. Many people have to survive on only three litres of water per day, and water from wells often does not taste good. Also, wells can be expensive to set up in regions which have problems with drought and floods.

Workbook answers

UNIT 4: Are there any monsters in the ocean?

A1

Adjective	Noun
Volcanic	Reef
Herbivorous	Mammal
Carnivorous	Dinosaur
Evaporating	Sea
Flowering	Plant
Extinct	Dinosaur
Continuous	Ocean
Metric	Measurement
Gigantic	Insect
Descending	Asteroid
Shallow	Sea

A2

a In the metric system, units <u>smaller</u> than a metre have <u>Latin</u> prefixes.

b In the metric system, units <u>larger</u> than a metre have <u>Greek</u> prefixes.

A3

millimetre
centimetre
decimetre
decametre
hectometre
kilometre

A4

a A metre equals 10 decimetres.

b A decametre equals 10 metres.

c A kilometre equals 1000 metres.

d A metre equals 1000 millimetres.

A5

a typical – usual, normal

b difference – change, distinction

c older – not younger, more ancient

d smaller – not bigger, tinier

e important – main, significant

f largest – biggest

A6

a What do you think is the <u>difference</u> between fresh water and sea water?

b If you evaporate water from a <u>typical</u> lake, you would get about 0.15 grams of salt.

c The world's oceans are split up into a number of <u>important</u> oceans and seas, (which are usually <u>smaller</u>).

d The Pacific Ocean is the <u>largest</u> body of water known to humans.

e Life within our oceans is far <u>older</u> than life on land.

B1 and B2

Look after – take care of
My mother looks after / takes care of her parents as well as her children.
Talk about – discuss
They are going to talk about / discuss our grades today.
Wait for – stay
They will only wait / stay for ten minutes and no more.
Worry about – be concerned about
He tends to worry about / be concerned about money a lot.
Concentrate on – focus on
You need to concentrate / focus more on your reading.
Drive through – travel
They drove /travelled through a very long underpass in Austria.

B3

We use the **past simple** tense with a <u>time reference</u> for past <u>actions</u>, states and facts, and for <u>repeated</u> past actions. Sometimes, the time reference may be <u>implied</u>, i.e. it is given somewhere else, for example in a previous sentence or phrase.

The **past perfect** tense is used to talk about an <u>event</u> that happened <u>before</u> another event in the past.

B4

a Michelle only <u>understood</u> the film because she <u>had read</u> the book.

b Mark <u>knew</u> the city so well because he <u>had visited</u> it several times before.

c Harry <u>had never been</u> to a live football match before last weekend.

d Chrystalla <u>visited</u> her friends' home just once while she was studying at university.

e Lorna <u>has applied</u> for the part-time job she saw advertised last week.

f My brother <u>had cooked</u> dinner for me when I <u>got</u> home last night.

g Justin and Greg <u>had finished</u> their homework only two minutes before the doorbell <u>rang</u>.

h Zak <u>knew</u> he needed glasses before he <u>had</u> his eyes checked.

C1

Nineteen times

C2

a Earth's land surface is about one seventh desert.

b Sub-tropical deserts are centred along the Tropics of Cancer and Capricorn.

c Desert air is dry.

d Deserts contain little or no vegetation.

e The Sahara Desert has unmoving sand dunes.

f The Arabian Desert covers almost the whole of the Arabian Peninsula.

g The Great Sandy Desert is located in the north of Western Australia.

C3

Precipitation = rain, snow or hail
Vegetation = plants in general
Dunes = hills of sand
Harsh conditions = being without vegetation

D1 Various possible answers

a The food was very hot and I couldn't eat it.

b It was a hot new company.

c Marcos is hot on video and PC games.

D2

Douglas Mawson, Belgrave Ninnis and Xavier Metz started out on their Antarctica expedition on 10th November 1912 and took the Far Eastern route. Things initially went well and they covered 478 kilometres in 35 days. But then disaster struck as Belgrave Ninnis, the likeable 25-year-old, fell down a crevasse with two dogs. For three hours the other men called for him but there was no reply. Not only had they lost a man and dogs, but also some very important supplies.

The men quickly pitched a spare tent and made the decision to return to base. Over the next few days they made good but slow progress as there were no longer any dogs to pull the sledges.

By 8th January Douglas Mawson was the only survivor of the team due to harsh conditions. He had to rush the last 160 kilometres because the ship to take him home was due to arrive on 15th January. He missed the ship by five hours and saw it sailing away. Fortunately, he was seen by a group of six men who had stayed behind to look for his team.

They had to stay in Antarctica for another ten months before the ship arrived to take them home. Mawson finally arrived home in February 1914, and later became a university professor, before completing two more Antarctic expeditions.

Workbook answers
UNIT 5: What's an ecosystem?

A1

a Mountainous
b Mediterranean
c Arid
d Polar
e Tropical
f Temperate

A2

a weak - Polar, b lack / shortage – Arid, c mild – Mediterranean, d humidity – Tropical, e strong / intense – Mountainous, f seasons - Temperate

A3

Across	Down
1. soup	2. prefix
5. ecosystem	3. vast
9. plant	4. herbivore
10. carnivore	6. imperative
11. suffix	7. grass
12. omnivore	8. grain

B3

The imperative is used to give an (a) instruction, a warning or a (b) command. It is formed by using the (c) base form of a verb without *to*, and without a (d) subject pronoun.

B4

a First, read and research about the type of lizard you want to live in your desert ecosystem.
b Next, buy everything you need: the lizard tank, rocks, sand, a heat lamp, a heat pad, a water bowl and, of course, the lizard!
c Then, place the heat pad under the tank.
d Make sure the aquarium is in a safe place where it won't get knocked over.
e After that, pour the sand into the tank.
f Next, place the rocks into the tank.
g Position the water bowl in the tank.
h Finally, place the heat lamp so that heat can only shine on one side of the tank.
i Gently put the lizard in its new home.

B1 and example answers for B2 (in *italics*)

PREFIXES	SUFFIXES
a de- opposite	**f** -ment state or condition, process of doing something
decrease – to go down	Document – an official letter or report
Sales have decreased this year, so we have less profit.	*The document was signed by everyone present.*
b dis- not, opposite	**g** -less without
disconnect – to cut off	Careless – without care or thinking
The electricity will be disconnected tonight.	*Christina is a very careless driver.*
c mis- wrong	**h** -s more than one
misbehave – to disobey, be naughty	Ships – more than one ship
Marios misbehaved and upset his sister.	*The ships are docking in the port.*
d non- not	**i** -able/-ible having a quality
nonsense – not logical, without meaning	Horrible – nasty, terrible
She talks a lot of nonsense, so ignore her.	*That was a horrible film!*
e semi - half	**j** -ness having characteristics of
semi-circle – half a circle	Suppleness – to be supple and move easily
All we could see was the semi-circle of the Moon.	*There was a suppleness to the leather.*
	k -ic can be done
	Generic – relating to, coming from
	Herbivore is a generic term for animals that only eat plants.

C1

a They're all about animals and a work placement
b 'c' because it describes the negative side as well
c A zoo, animal sanctuary, safari park, etc
d Wild, injured, orphaned animals
e various answers possible

C2 – sample 'good' answer

Dear Sir/Madam,
I am 16 years old and go to high school and I would like to work as a volunteer at the sanctuary.
I have worked with donkeys near my village, where I looked after all the animals on a farm, feeding them and cleaning their living areas. In some cases I also exercised the animals.
I am free at weekends and also the school holidays, but not during exam times.
I have always had a pet at home, and I enjoy being with animals. I am very lucky as my father is a vet, and sometimes I have the chance to work with him.
Please could you tell me the address of the sanctuary and also the hours you would need me to work?
Many thanks
Patty

Workbook answers
UNIT 6: Can bees scare elephants?

A1

a bear – A large furry mammal that lives in the wild.
b cat – A small mammal that can be both domesticated or wild.
c chicken – A bird that has feathers but does not fly.
d dolphin – A mammal that lives in the sea and is highly intelligent
e frog – An amphibian that lives in water but can also be found on land.
f human - A mammal that lives on land but also wants to live in space.
g mouse – A mammal that is very shy and often chased by cats.
h rabbit – A mammal that people often keep as pets, but is also found living in the wild.
i shark – A fish mammal that lives in the sea and eats smaller fish.
j sheep – A mammal that lives on farms and provides wool and meat.
k spider – An arthropod that can be dangerous, and which some people are frightened of.
l wolf – A mammal that looks like a dog but is wild.

A2 This exercise can be done by process of elimination!
Advise students to count the number of letters in each word

From the top down: MENACE / NARRATOR / FRUITLESS / BETRAY / HARPOONIST / NAVAL / SUBMARINE / CONSTANTLY
New word: NAUTILUS

A3

Sea monster
Marine biologist
Ocean liner
Electrically powered track
Enigmatic creator
Noted down

A4 – various answers possible

A5

a Malaria
b Malfunctions
c Malcontent
d Malformed
e Malevolent

B1

a Konrad admitted <u>taking</u> the money.
b Ravinder said that she and her family had enjoyed <u>eating</u> at the new restaurant.
c Joshua agreed <u>to help</u> his father paint the kitchen.
d Otis narrowly avoided <u>hitting</u> the tree.
e Cho and Rebekah arranged <u>to meet</u> at the cinema.
f Rae denied <u>taking</u> Yvonne's CDs.
g Shelly was asked not <u>to speak</u> so loudly.
h They can't afford <u>to go</u> on holiday this summer.
i They decided not <u>to work</u> because of the bad weather.
j Satish failed <u>to understand</u> the equation in his maths lesson.

B2

to + infinitive	-ing
fail	miss
learn	recommend
manage	suggest
need	
promise	
refuse	
want	

B3 – various answers possible

B4

a to study
b to decide
c to refuse
d asking
e to give
f to work
g holding
h cuddling
i to go
j to travel
k working
l to do

B5

a These invertebrates are special, aren't they?
b You're not serious, are you?
c Jellyfish and worms have no eyes, do they?
d Spiders are not insects, are they?
e Nobody has ever seen a living giant squid, have they?

B6

a *Twenty Thousand Leagues Under the Sea* was written by Jules Verne, wasn't it?
b The story is told by one of the passengers, isn't it?
c The expedition sets sail from Long Island, doesn't it?
d The three protagonists are thrown overboard, aren't they?
e The narrator had no idea how they survived the storm, did he?
f Nobody knows what happened to the *Nautilus*, do they?

C1

English	Arabic	Greek	German	Latin
duck bull	giraffe	hippopotamus rhinoceros shark elephant python crocodile	poodle dog	leopard shark salmon trout elephant

C2

Behaviour	Appearance	Greek
duck	giraffe	elephant
hippopotamus	rhinocerous	python
poodle	leopard	
bull	shark	
salmon	crocodile	
trout		

D1 – various answers possible

D2

a How long have we predicted the weather for?
   For as long as humans have lived.
b Why was it important in early times to predict the weather?
   Because it was a factor for survival.
c How did people use to understand the weather?
   Through the observation of animals, birds and insects.

d What do meteorologists do today?
   They use computers.
e How accurate are they?
   Not 100%.
d What influences them?
   Warming of the oceans and planets.
e Are computers more effective than animals at prediction?
   No, animals are because it's linked to natural survival instincts.

Workbook answers
UNIT 7: Can penguins see under water?

A1

a sight / eyes
b touch / hands
c taste / tongue
d smell / nose
e hearing / ears

A2

a sight / eyes / sky
b hands / touch / cat
c tongue / taste / fruit
d nose / smell / grass
e ears / listen / song

A3 – various answers possible

A4 and A5

rfgadoynl – dragonfly (a)
futbytrle – butterfly (b)
ylf – fly (c)
acmnoelhe – chameleon (d)
nta – ant (e)
umsoe - mouse (f)
geael – eagle (g)
sjlflheyi – jellyfish (h)
baibtr – rabbit (i)

B1

a Dragonflies see much better than humans do.
b Bats are able to see more clearly than people can.
c Many fish move faster through water than animals on land.
d Chameleons can move their eyes more independently than other animals.
e Insects sense things more easily than humans do.
f Butterflies use their wings more efficiently than birds do.

B2 – various answers possible

B3

The -*ing* form of a verb can be used as a (a) noun. It is common after certain (b) verbs, while other verbs are followed by the (c) infinitive form; some verbs can be followed by either (d) -*ing* or an infinitive. Sometimes a (e) gerund can be the (f) subject of a sentence or the (g) object of a preposition. Notice that when (h) *by* is followed by an -*ing* form, it tells us (i) how something is done.

C1

	Name	Function
Top layer	Neocortex	Thinking Creativity and logic
Middle layer	Limbic layer	Controls our emotions Deals with sense of identity and beliefs, and with our long-term memory.
Bottom layer	Reptilian	Survival Body's functions and instincts

C2

a features – characteristics
b part or side – hemisphere
c sensible – logical
d involving original or imaginative ideas – creative
e producing a positive result – effective

D1

a Cheetah, pronghorn antelope, greyhound, red kangaroo, snakehead fish, African elephant, grizzly bear and gorilla
b Usain Bolt, David Rushida, Mike Powell and Javier Sotomayor.
c Cheetah
d Usain Bolt
e Gorilla
f No name given

D2

Sport	Olympian	Achievement	Animal	Achievement
Running	Usain Bolt	100 metres in 9.58 seconds	Cheetah	5.8 seconds
	(a) David Rushida	(b) 800 metres in 1 minute 41 seconds	Pronghorn antelope	(c) 33 seconds
Jumping	Mike Powell	(d) 8.95 metres	(e) Kangaroo	(f) 12.8 metres
	(g) Javier Sotomayor	high jump 2.45 metres	(h) Snakehead fish	(i) 4 metres
Weightlifting			African elephant	lift 300 kg carry 820 kg
			(j) Grizzly bear	(k) 455 kg
			(l) Gorilla	(m) 900 Kg

D3 – various answers possible

Workbook answers
UNIT 8: How hot are chilli peppers?

A1

Across:	Down:
2. edible	1.cultivated
3. indigenous	5.loaded
4. mild	6.potent
7. boosts	8.calories
10.relieve	9. minimal
11.trigger	12. indoors
13.sweat	

A2

a edible
b indoors
c minimal
d relieve
e calories
f sweat
g mild
h cultivated
i indigenous
j potent
k trigger
l loaded
m boosts

A3 Suggested answers

Positive connotation	Negative connotation
delicate	beanpole
featherweight	beanstalk
fragile	bony
lean	pole
lightweight	skeletal
slight	skinny
slim	stick
small	undernourished
	underweight

A4

a He doesn't eat anything and looks undernourished.
b She's got very delicate features and is the perfect shape for a dancer.
c She's very fragile now and uses a walking stick to get about.
d The children's skinny shape makes them look younger than they are.
e She's quite small for her age, particularly compared to her sister's (OR sisters') size.
f He's as tall as a beanpole and wears his brother's (OR brothers') clothes, which are too small for him.

B1

Paragraph	Word/phrase	What it refers to
1	All of them	Hundreds of rainforest plants
2	Our	Modern medicine
3	Such plants	Tropical rainforest plants
4	The fruit	Peach palm
5	Them	Plant species used as medicine

B2

Joachim and his sister used to live in the city and travel every day by train to school. It used to take *them* about an hour each way and (a) they used to arrive home feeling dirty and tired. Also, because (b) their mother worked in an office in the city, (c) they didn't get to see (d) her until late in the evening. By the time (e) she got home, it was very late and everybody was hungry, but (f) nobody/no one wanted to cook. This meant (g) they had to buy fast food or something that was ready-made. Over time, (h) their diet affected (i) their health. (j) They decided to move to the countryside and bought a small house and went to a local school. In the countryside, (k) they lived a better life and ate a better diet!

B3

a Joachim and his sister
b Joachim and his sister's
c Joachim and his sister
d Their mother
e Their mother
f Joachim, his sister, their mother
g The family
h The family's
i The family's
j The family
k The family

B4

a The teacher hasn't given us many essays to write this term.

b How much material are they expecting us to research for the project?

c Unfortunately, he's already had a few / many problems with the new car.

d There are too many weeds in the garden.

e She didn't use a lot of / much butter in her cake and that made a difference.

f He's paid very little attention in the class.

g It's only rained a few times this year.

h How much do most people do to help charities?

i A lot/Most of the advice the teacher gave has been helpful.

j He only gave a little help after promising so much.

k He's great with computers and few people know as much as he does.

C1

a i) They come in all shapes, sizes and colours.
   ii) More than 400 different types are grown.
   iii) They are easy to cultivate.

b No set answer.

c Chilli con carne, curry

d No set answer.

e You would burn your eyes and skin.

C2

(a) Fry the mince, green peppers, onions, chilli powder and black pepper until the meat is brown.

(b) Add the tomato juice and beans and

(c) cook everything.

(d) Top with sour cream or yoghurt.

(e) Serve with rice or naan bread.

C3 and C4 – various answers possible

Workbook answers
UNIT 9: Who was Ibn Battuta?

A1

a I understood that he said we should 'call' him not 'visit' him.

b He slowly found his way through the crowds of people to reach his destination.

c She loves to travel around when she goes to different countries; she's not the sort of person who just sits on a beach.

d He went by boat all along the coast rather than travel by train.

e They were shown the pyramids and given a good history lesson.

f Because of the bad weather, it took them two days to go up the mountain.

g They finally found the site they had spent many years looking for.

h She tried to get to the top of the mountain, but had no energy left.

i They finally came to an agreement on how much they should pay.

A2 – various answers possible

B1

Countries that end in –*land* and –*a*	Nationalities that end in –*ese* and –*ian*	Languages that end in –*ian* and –*n*
Greenland	Chinese	Latvian
Swaziland	Portuguese	Norwegian
Neverland	Maltese	Estonian
Nigeria	Canadian	Albanian
Botswana	Zambian	German
Samoa	Malaysian	Armenian
Australia	Egyptian	Hawaiian

B2 Example answers

a The kitchen had flooded.
The furniture had been destroyed.

b She had torn my magazine.
She had broken my lamp.

c It had eaten the food on the table.
It had made the floor dirty.

d She had been away for three days.
She had not cooked the lunch.

C1 – various answers possible

C2

1 F: Wind power
2 D: Today's technology
3 C: Spaceships with sails
4 B: Inter-planet transport
5 E: Warp speed
6 A: Even faster

C3

Paragraph 1: a new world / 15th and 16th centuries / steam engines
Paragraph 2: better technologies / rowing
Paragraph 3:
Paragraph 4:
Paragraph 5: scientists dream
Paragraph 6: several years younger / time slows down

C4

a enormous = very large, huge
b current = of today, contemporary
c ancestors = people from previous generations
d immense = vast, massive
e solar = related to sun
f whisk = carry swiftly
g descendants = people from future generations
h marvel = wonder
i authors = writers
j debate = discussion

D1

a It is the exploration of cave systems.

D2

a Cricket
b Crawlway
c Cave
d Formation
e Canyon
f Strenuous

D3 – various answers possible

Workbook answers

UNIT 10: What's the best job for a teenager?

A1

bike courier - delivers packages around a city
cat food quality controller - smells and feels animal food
hippotherapist - uses horses to help people with disabilities
ethical hacker - makes sure companies' software is secure
Brazilian mosquito researcher - tries to find treatments for malaria
monkey chaser - works in a safari park to stop monkeys escaping
Buckingham Palace guard - stands without moving for hours
Feng Shui consultant - arranges furniture for the best flow of energy

A2

a <u>Severe shortages</u> of milk prevented many dairy products from being produced.
b The <u>likelihood</u> of <u>brutal</u> violence hindered the TV crew from covering the story fully.
c There is a <u>constant</u> supply of renewable <u>timber</u> from Norway.
d There are <u>substantial criteria</u> on which to base your job application.
e It is <u>desirable</u> to have a good <u>proficiency</u> in English for the job.

B1

a He invited me to go to the cinema with him tonight/ that night.
b He promised to bring back /return my book tomorrow/ the next day.
c He warned me not to be late again or I'd lose my job.
d She accused me of taking her bag.
e They complained that the same student was / is always asked the answers.
f He recommended that we should try the restaurant as the food was / is excellent.
g He denied stealing her bag as he hadn't been / wasn't in the room.
h He suggested that I take / took the bus instead of driving.

B2

She asked if I had applied for the job of travel representative.
I answered that I had and that I had specifically asked to be based in Greece because I can speak fluent Greek.
She asked if I had ever been to Greece and specifically the Peloponnisos area.
I answered that I had been to Greece but I didn't know that area very well and was more familiar with northern Greece.
She said that shouldn't be a problem and asked what I thought would be one of the biggest issues with this job
I replied that the hours were quite long and not very regular.
She asked if I would be available to work overtime.
I replied that I would be.
She asked what I thought of the salary and if I thought it was reasonable.
I said it was fine as I knew I would earn commission as well.

B3

a <u>Probably</u> he won't be with us next year, as he's moved on to a different job.
b <u>Obviously</u> they won't be coming with us, as they're not here yet.
c <u>Unsurprisingly</u> they have no interest in the music, as it's from a different generation.
d <u>Luckily</u> I went to the shop early and they hadn't sold out of milk.
e <u>Exactly</u>! That's what I asked you to do because I knew how he would react.
f <u>Definitely</u> count me in. I would love to come with you.
g <u>Sadly</u>, no he won't make it, as he's already running late.
h <u>Absolutely</u>! We'd love to help at the charity event.
i <u>Certainly</u> yes! He would be an excellent asset to the team, so include him.

C1 Various answers possible

a 750 hours of structured learning A
b air guitar B
c airline A
d aviation law A
e blockbuster B

f equipment A/B
g fashion shoots B
h Hollywood B
i intensive training A/B
j programme A/B
k lot of standing around A/B
l meteorology A
m Royal Air Force A
n superstardom B
o world tour A/B

C2

Average - normal, usual
Blockbuster - best-seller
Brush up - revise, practise
Consistently - regularly
Intensive - needing a lot of effort
Obtain - get
Occupations - jobs
Undergo - follow

C4

a Since the 1940's.
b 750 hours of structured learning and 150 hours of flight training
c Meteorology and aviation law
d Theatre acting and blockbusters
e Because 90% of the time will be out of work.

D1 Various answers possible

D2

Dear Michael,
I wish to apply for the job in the newspaper for the coffee shop. I have not worked in a coffee shop before but since you give training, I hope that will not be a problem. I have got good English because I have been going to special English classes at the university. I like talking to people and I think that will be important to your customers.
I am satisfied with the salary and conditions.
I hope to hear from you soon.
With regards
Michelle

D3

Dear Jane,
I wish to apply for the library administrative job which I recently saw advertised.
I would be available to work the 20 hours a week during the months of June and July. I have good knowledge of English and also satisfactory computer skills.
I am a person who likes to work in a quiet environment, particularly if I am surrounded by books.
I look forward to hearing from you about my application.
Best regards,

Workbook answers
UNIT 11: Who are the Maasai?

A1 Various answers possible

A2 and A3

a bungee jumping
b marathon running
c swamp football
d underwater rugby
e apple race
f goat pulling
g canoe jumping
h land diving
I potato wrestling
j tuna throwing
k indoor kite-flying

A4

Column A	Column B	Column C	Column D
Tendons	Athens	Latvian Warrior	Shoe
Bones	Kenya	Maasai	Footwear
Ligaments	Sahara	Runner	iPads
Muscles	Tanzania	Soldier	Credit cards

Column A describes parts of the body.
Column B describes names of places.
Column C describes types of people.
Column D describes objects.

B1

Verb	Noun	Adjective	Adverb
	commoner	common	commonly
absorb	absorption	absorbed	
provide	provider / provision	provided	
	entirety	entire	entirely
exceed	excess	excessive	excessively
stabilise	stability	stable	
sever	severity	severe	severely
encourage	encouragement	encouraged	encouragingly

B2 – various answers possible

B3

a She loved the concert. The <u>singing</u> was excellent.
b That's her favourite lesson. The <u>teaching</u> is always very good.
c Please throw your gum away. <u>Chewing</u> in class is so rude.
d He's the best modern artist. His <u>painting</u> is so colourful.
e Young people don't have much money. Their <u>spending</u> is very limited.
f <u>Driving</u> at night can be quite stressful.
g Don't believe what she says. Her <u>lying</u> is constant nowadays.
h <u>Playing</u> with my friends is my favourite pastime.
i <u>Waiting</u> for them at the restaurant was not a good idea.
j She walked into the room <u>carrying</u> a heavy bag.

C1 & C2 – various answers possible

C2 actual answers

120 metres under water – Paragraph B
aerodynamic suits – Paragraph D
broken bones – Paragraph J
can still be dangerous – Paragraph J
cave creature – Paragraph C

divers are well trained – Paragraph C

fly in the air – Paragraph G

handlebars – Paragraph G

highly modified skateboards – Paragraph I

incredibly dangerous sport – Paragraph A

it's not exactly legal – Paragraph A

massive waves – Paragraph E

non-motorised sport – Paragraph D

not getting enough oxygen – Paragraph B

pavement – Paragraph I

pirates – Paragraph H

sharks – Paragraph H

tides – Paragraph E

try to hang on – Paragraph F

very dangerous – Paragraph J

C3

a BASE jumping

b free diving

c cave diving

d speed skiing

e rock fishing

f bull riding

g supercross

h solo yacht racing

i street luging

j bike riding

D1 – various answers possible

i. Makes their lives exciting

ii. Makes them try different sports

iii. Challenges them

iv. Makes them aware of risks and dangers

v. Tests them mentally

D3 – example answer

I agree with the writer of the blog because I think that a child should be challenged. It is good to try different sports as all we hear about are the normal everyday sports that people play, like football and tennis. There are so many other sports that a child should try. They might find they have the skills that a sport like football does not have.

I don't agree with the writer though when she says 'forget the dangers'. If you choose to do a sport and are aware of the dangers to yourself, then that is fine but not if you have an accident and then involve other people. Children should do 'mild' extreme sports until they are mature enough to understand and respect their body more.

Workbook answers
UNIT 12: What does a triathlete do?

A1

What/name?	Football	Cricket	Badminton
Where/play?	On a pitch	Cricket pitch	Badminton court
When/play?	Various days/times	Anytime	Anytime
What/equipment?	Ball / goal posts /flags	Bat / ball / wickets	Shuttlecock / racquets
How many/players?	11 each team	11 each team	Two / four
Aim/game?	To get the most goals	To score runs	Score points
How/win?	By scoring most goals	By scoring the most runs	Scoring most points

A2 – various answers possible

A3

a These days, you sweat less in sports clothes because they have better <u>ventilation</u> and <u>absorb moisture properly</u>.
b They now make <u>two-piece body suits</u> for women that are very comfortable.
c The sofa was covered in a <u>thick, long-lasting, lightweight</u> material.
d If they continue at their <u>current speed</u>, the time will be better than last year's record.
e If you are <u>measured</u>, then the suit should be a <u>better fit</u>.
f 'If you'd learn to tell the time, then maybe you'd be a <u>better time-keeper</u>!'
g The suit was an <u>excellent fit</u> and did not hang off him like the other style did.

B1 – various answers possible

i Go Fast Pro is available in more colours than Leisure Extra.
ii Leisure Pro is cheaper for adults than Go Fast Pro.
iii Go Fast Pro has got more sizes for adults and children than Leisure Extra.
iv Leisure Extra's running shoes are heavier than Go Fast Pro's.
v Go Fast Pro's running shoes are more available than Leisure Extra's.
vi Leisure Extra's running shoes can be used for more purposes than Go Fast Pro's.

B2 – various answers possible

B3

a You can buy quite cheap wetsuits these days, <u>but</u> the problem is that they tend to be made of thick material which is not very flexible. <u>Unfortunately,</u> this makes body movement quite difficult.
b Goggles are really important; <u>however,</u> the shape and how much you spend is up to you.
c <u>Nevertheless,</u> these may be a good option for swimmers who use contact lenses.
d <u>Moreover,</u> they are more aerodynamic and <u>consequently</u> offer better ventilation for the wearer.
e <u>Additionally,</u> if your feet are soft and susceptible to blisters, you should invest in a good pair of socks that can absorb moisture properly.

B4

a When is he <u>going to</u> compete in the next race?
b Lie down quietly and rest: that <u>will</u> help your headache.
c The nominations for the next Olympic Games are <u>going to</u> be announced soon.
d He <u>is meeting</u> some friends after work
e The train only <u>leaves</u> when all the seats are full.
f They <u>will</u> carry your bag if it is too heavy.
g I <u>will be seeing</u> the headteacher later today.

C1 – various answers possible

C2

lodge – small building, often in a forest or jungle
canals – waterways
trails – paths or tracks
daring – brave

C3 – various answers possible

a banana plantations – large area where bananas are grown
b bird's eye view – to be able to see something from above
c fireworks display – entertainment provided by fireworks
d hot springs – natural hot water from the ground
e interactive exhibits – exhibits, maybe in a museum, that you can touch and use
f narrow waterways – not wide rivers or canals
g rafting trip – a short journey on a flat boat made of wood

C5

a interactive exhibits
b narrow waterways
c banana plantations
d rafting trip
e hot springs
f fireworks display
g bird's eye view

D1 – various answers possible

D2 – example answer

Moon golf has got to be the most exciting future sport ever. Imagine travelling to the moon to take part in a game of golf where the craters are where the ball has to be shot. Because the craters are so far apart, you would have moon buggies to get you around and, when you got out of the buggy, imagine bouncing around from spot to spot chasing the ball.

D3

a What's the name of the sport?
Hover boarding.
b Where is the sport played?
Anywhere.
c When is it played?
Any time
d What equipment is used?
All you need is a hover board and the boots attached to it.

e How many players are there?
There is no set number.
f What is the aim of the game?
To be skilful.
g How do you win?
By being the most skilful hover boarder.

A1

a The World around us is made up of chemicals.
b Scientists have discovered about 120 chemicals.
c The Moon's gravity pulls the water in the earth's oceans.
d Languages are not static; they are dynamic.
e English has borrowed from about 120 different languages.
f Humans use only about 0.3% of the earth's water.

A2

a temperature
b poor hygiene
c sweat
d water vapour
e weight
f freeze
g fish tank
h fruit and vegetables
i health problems
j sinks and toilets

A3

a They have a very unhealthy diet and do not eat any <u>fruit and vegetables</u>.
b The <u>sinks and toilets</u> in the school need to be cleaned more often, as they are used by many children.
c The world's <u>temperature</u> is rising and many places are experiencing water shortages.
d You need to keep a check on your <u>weight</u> and make sure it is stable.
e Men tend to <u>sweat</u> much more than women when exercising.
f They will <u>freeze</u>, as they did not take very many clothes with them.
g <u>Poor hygiene</u> is an area that should be taught more in school.
h Their <u>fish tank</u> is full of some very exotic types now and they have spent a lot of money on it.
i <u>Water vapour</u> often results in rain, but not enough in some countries.
j <u>Health problems</u> later in life can often be prevented if you respect your body when you are young.

A4

a <u>scientist</u> chemicals
b recognise <u>equivalent</u>
c <u>bilingual</u> dictionary
d <u>reference</u> sources
e <u>definitions</u> organism
f properties <u>artificial</u>
g <u>interact</u> aluminium
h discovered <u>attraction</u>
i <u>electromagnets</u> nucleus
j <u>equivalent bilingual</u>

A5

Electromagnets
Interact
Equivalent
Reference
Scientist
Artificial
Substances
Bilingual
Definitions
Attraction
Mauritania

A6

a etiquette
b couch potato
c audiophile
d e -ruitment
e freemale
f buzzword
g app
h fashionista
i hoody
j chillaxing
k chatroom
l cyber café

B1

a Two hundred people are employed by the car manufacturer in our town.
c Running water was supplied to all villages by an international charity.

B2

a About 70% of Earth's surface <u>is covered</u> with <u>water</u>.
b Water <u>is made</u> up of two elements: <u>hydrogen</u> and oxygen.
c Water <u>is delivered</u> to people's <u>homes</u> by the water industry.
d Ocean tides <u>are caused</u> by the rotation of the <u>Earth</u>.
e Water from the sea <u>contains</u> <u>salt</u>.
f Seawater <u>is made</u> up of about 35 grams of dissolved <u>salt</u> for every kilogram of seawater
g <u>Oil</u> separates from water when it <u>is mixed</u> together.
h Drinking water <u>is known</u> by humans to avoid <u>dehydration</u>.
i Water <u>is used</u> in agricultural <u>irrigation</u> to grow crops.
j Water <u>is needed</u> frequently by fire fighters to extinguish <u>fires</u>.

B3

Verb	Noun	Adjective	Adverb
limit	limit	limited	limitlessly
discover	discovery	discoverable	
differ	difference	different	differently
include	inclusion	inclusive	inclusively
combine	combination	combined	
exert	exertion	exerted	
depend	dependant	dependable	dependably
shorten	shortage	short	shortly
power	power	powerful	powerfully

B4

a A <u>combination</u> of water and salt makes up the world's seawater.
b The <u>short</u> supply of water in many countries is a serious future concern.
c The waterfall surged <u>powerfully</u>, producing an amazing force of energy.
d To <u>include</u> water conservation in a biology lesson's curriculum is sensible.
e The villagers <u>depend</u> very much on the one water supply in the village.
f The <u>different</u> flavours in the food made it extremely tasty.
g Some areas of the world have huge <u>shortages</u>, whereas others have an excess.
h The <u>discovery</u> of penicillin changed the face of medical development.

i She is very <u>dependable</u> and looks after the home when her parents are away.
j 'If you <u>exert</u> a bit more energy, you'll probably find it easier to open.'

C1, C2 and C3 – various answers possible

C4

Diarrhoea and cholera – d
20–50 litres – b
11% - c

C6

a True
b False
c False
d True
e True
f True
g False
h True

D1 – various answers possible

D2 – example answer

The Shedoof is used to raise water from one level to another. It is operated by hand where one end is a pole and the other end is a weight. Egyptians built canals to improve irrigation because more land needed water. Buckets were filled with water and the weight then raised the bucket. The Shedoof is still used today, particularly in Egypt and the Near East. It can provide over 2500 litres of water per day from a maximum water depth of 3 metres. The bucket is made of animal skin and can hold about 20 litres of water.

Workbook answers
UNIT 14: How important is oil?

A1 (Other answers possible)

a <u>glasses</u> credit card table phone
  They are not a rectangular shape.

b <u>taxi</u> police car ambulance fire engine
  Used for public transport.

c whale dolphin seal <u>octopus</u>
  The only sea animal with legs.

d <u>smaller</u> more efficient more popular more energetic
  The only comparative adjective without 'more'.

e pad pencil <u>book</u> pen
  The word begins with a 'b'.

f email SMS <u>fax</u> apps
  An outmoded form of technology.

g planned painted <u>lost</u> dialled
  An irregular past tense verb.

h currently presently now <u>formerly</u>
  Means 'before'.

i lens eye glasses <u>audio</u>
  To do with the ears.

j circle oval round <u>wheel</u>
  Not a shape but an object.

A2

a How important to us in our daily lives is oil?

b Many manufactured items are made from oil.

c Many animals are seriously injured because of plastic litter.

d How many barrels of oil are used daily?

e In 1983 the first mobile phone was sold to the public.

f Mobile phones were more a symbol of status than a convenience.

g We should write the word when a number is ten or smaller.

h Glasses developed from just a lens frame in one eye .

i Some people say the most important invention is the wheel.

j The modern contact lens is 120 years old.

A3

a The <u>invention</u> of the phone revolutionised people's lives.

b The sweets tasted so <u>synthetic</u> that even the children couldn't eat them.

c The <u>extent</u> to which people speak English as a Second Language is vast.

d Pizza tastes much better if cooked in a clay <u>oven.</u>

e Measles have become <u>widespread</u> again because people have chosen not to vaccinate.

f Rice is a very <u>versatile</u> grain, as it can be used with anything.

g The pots are <u>moulded</u> by hand and so each one is different.

h The prices <u>rocketed</u> when it was seen how popular the apps were.

i People have been driving for <u>decades</u> now and will never give up the car.

j Many people <u>emigrated</u> from Ireland when there was a potato famine.

k Many elephants have been killed for their tusks to supply the <u>ivory</u> market.

B1

What time does the film start? There is a show at 18.00 and again at 20.30.

How much do the tickets cost? It depends. If you're an adult $8 and $6 if you're a child.

Who are the actors? Nobody famous. There are some unknown names.

Why didn't they use anyone famous? Don't know. Suppose it was cheaper.

When does the next film come out? It should be here next week.

How will I find out? We'll put the information on our website.

Where can I get the address from? I'll give it to you. It's www …

B2 – other answers possible

a Who is going on the school trip?
  All the teachers and classes.

b When is the school trip?
  It's next week.

c What time are they coming back?
  I think 19.30, but you'd better check.

d Who's bringing the food?
  Well, every class has to do something. I think our class is bringing the cakes.

e Why are you celebrating?
  I think because it's the school's anniversary. It's ten years old!

f Are you going?
How much does it cost?
Yes, I think so. It won't be much – about $5.

g Where is it going to be held?
In the sports' hall, because it's nice and big.

h How are you getting there?
I'll get my dad to take me. Do you want to come with us?

B3 – various answers possible

a Since = present perfect
b Today = present simple / present perfect / going to
c Last week = past simple
d Last night = past simple
e Come now! = present simple
f At the weekend = present simple / past simple
g The month before last = past perfect / past simple
h This week – present perfect / going to
i Presently = present simple / going to
j The day before yesterday = past simple
k Lately = present perfect
l After = past simple / present simple
m Yet = present perfect / present simple

B4 – various answers possible

C1 – various answers possible

a cruising altitude – how high an object flies
b founded – when it was started
c tirelessly – with a lot of effort
d predecessor – the person before
e flying saucer – an alien space craft
f altitudes – heights
g gained – to obtain
h fins and pods – group names of sea mammals
i 120 horsepower – energy of a car
j hazard – a danger
k feasible – possible
l parachute – an umbrella shaped material used to float to Earth
m viable – practical

C2

a congestion – traffic jams
b vision – idea
c people you work with – colleagues
d very intelligent people – geniuses
e information – knowledge
f unusual – looks like something from a sci-fi movie
g predictions, guesses – future projections
h break down – systems fail
i possible – viable

C3

Moller's company set up in (a) 1983.
VTOL = (b) Vertical Take-off and Landing
M200x made in (c) 1989.
Main problem with M200x is (d) slow speed.
M400 gets power from (e) eight small 120-horsepower Rotapower engines and it can travel at speeds up to (f) 500 kilometres per hour with a (g) range of 1500 kilometres.
M400 engines produce less (h) pollution than normal car engines.
City buildings may provide (i) vertiports for Skycars in the future.
Little chance of overcrowding because (j) skycars would be 2 kilometres away from other vehicles.

D1

Thanks to
… if not easier
…was put to good use
…give a better performance
One of the best things…
…like a dream

D2 – various answers possible

D3 – example answer

When we think of science-fiction films and books, not many of their predictions become reality, and neither will the M400 Skycar. Imagine people who live in flats, for example, they do not all have an individual flat roof, so where will they park their skycars? Imagine the cost of producing such a vehicle and the infrastructure that would be needed for such vehicles to exist in our urban areas. What would happen to all the roads and cars that have taken years to build and all the money spent to repair them?

A1

a a thousand years - millennium
b tale, narrative - story
c formation - creation
d era, age - period
e old-fashioned - quaint
f timid, reluctant - backward
g not cultured - uncivilised
h whole - entire
i ice house - igloo
j flyover - bridge
k small church - chapel
l welcome desk - reception
m colonisers - settlers
n food seekers - hunters
o theorist - philosopher
p from the same era - contemporaries
q disorder - chaos
r fast-flowing water - rushing rapids
s environmental tragedy - natural disaster
t destructive flow - crashing torrent

A2

Greek and English

A3

a quaint
b hunters
c millennium
d natural disasters
e entire
f reception
g crashing torrent
h contemporaries

A4

a 1377 m – one thousand, three hundred and seventy seven million
b 5850 m – five thousand eight hundred and fifty million
c 2004 – two thousand and four
d 1894 – one thousand eight hundred and ninety-four
e 1982 – one thousand nine hundred and eighty-two
f 50,080,310 – fifty million eighty thousand three hundred and ten

g 67,356 – sixty seven thousand three hundred and fifty-six
h 1,372,896 – one million three hundred and seventy-two thousand eight hundred and ninety-six

B1

a The fruit needs to _soften_ because it is too hard to eat.
b We need to _strengthen_ her up, as she is very weak after her illness.
c The puppy is very _weak_ because he's not had any water for days.
d They should use _less_ water when they wash up, as it's wasteful.
e She took a sip of water to _moisten_ her throat.
f The little girl smiled at her aunt _sweetly_ when she gave her a kiss.
g The fruit on the trees quickly _ripened_ in the warm sunshine.
h The sky was soon _dark_ and it was a sign that bad weather was coming.

B2

a The children need to quieten down, as they're very noisy.
b You need to lengthen those trousers, as they're too short.
c That shirt is very tight on the neck, loosen it!
d That soup does look very nice. I think you should thicken it a bit, though.
e You need to widen that door frame, otherwise the door won't fit.
f If you drink milk when you're a child, it will strengthen your bones.
g Fasten the dog to the tree and then it won't run away.
h The day will brighten later, as the forecast is a clear sky.

B3

Hi

Had the ultimate experience when I visited London recently, as went to see Tower Bridge. It was an absolute pleasure to see it for real, as have always seen it in pictures only. I did the complete tour of the place and walked around in total disbelief, as it's such a cool bridge. The mechanics of the place are an utter dream for an engineer, and I got the man who worked there to explain the entire system to me.

George Peters
21 Kailykli Street,
Upper Kambia
Nicosia
1223
Cyprus

C1

a array - collection
b curved - rounded
c goals - aims
d harbour - port, marina
e high-rise buildings - very tall structures, skyscrapers
f lagoon - small lake
g mimics - copies
h sloping - higher on one side
i smog – pollution
j sustainable - does not destroy the environment
k tracks - path of a railway

C2

a high-rise buildings
b curved
c array
d tracks
e lagoon
f smog
g goals
h sloping
i harbour
j sustainable
k mimics

C3

a The Urban cactus
b The Treescraper Tower of Tomorrow
c The Anti-smog building and the Ascent at Roebling Bridge
d The Anti-smog building

D1 – example answer

In 2007, some children were on a school excursion when an awful accident happened. The bridge which their bus was travelling over, namely the 1-35W Mississippi bridge, collapsed. The bus was hanging over the side when the back door opened and the hero, Mr Hernandez, managed to get all of the children out, resulting in their having no more than minor injuries and none needing hospitalisation.

C2

In the summer of 2007 there were 61 children in the bus with adults. They were tired and on their way home from a school excursion at a water park. While they were being driven over the 1-35W Mississippi bridge, the eight-lane, steel bridge collapsed. The back door of the bus was kicked open by their summer programme's sports coordinator, Mr Hernandez, who then passed the kids out, resulting in only 16 needing hospitalisation.

Workbook answers

UNIT 16: Where are the Seven Wonders of the Ancient World?

A1

a The Temple of Artemis.
b The Statue of Zeus.
c The Great Pyramid of Giza.
d The Lighthouse of Alexandria.
e The Mausoleum of Halicarnassus.
f The Hanging Gardens of Babylon.
g The Colossus of Rhodes.

A2

a The Great Pyramid of Giza.
b The Hanging Gardens of Babylon.
c The Temple of Artemis
d The Statue of Zeus.
e The Mausoleum of Halicarnassus.
f The Colossus of Rhodes.
g The Lighthouse of Alexandria.

A3

a stone's throw away
b colossal
c vibrant
d knick-knacks
e stroll along
f culinary sensation
g chirping
h scurrying
i iconic
j bumper-to-bumper
k hawkers
l morning catch

B1

a ... believed to be given ...
b ... it was thought to be established ...
c ... was said to be fortified ...
d ...was reported to be destroyed ...
e ...was claimed to be abandoned ...

B2 – various answers possible

a The thief is believed to have been robbing other houses in the street.
b Many marine animals are thought to have been killed in badly placed fishing nets.

c The painting is thought to have been destroyed in the fire.
d Beautiful buildings are said to have been destroyed by earthquakes.
e The painting is believed to have been stolen before the exhibition.
f They are thought to have been injured while climbing the mountain.

B3

a It's a shame she has resigned from her job.
b It's upsetting that you don't want me to come.
c I'm glad you're feeling much better.
d I'm sorry she's so upset.
e She told me that she hadn't got the scholarship.
f He believes that it's a good price for children.
g He has guessed that you're leaving.
h She agrees that she's been very silly.

C1 – various answers possible – and C2

C *History*
f romance, adventure and pleasure
h snowdrifts

A *Carriage*
b cosy confines
g Sleeping Car 3309

D *Life on board*
d panoramic views
e personal steward

B *Dining*
a afternoon tea
c French silverware

C3

a i. In 1929 it was stuck in a snow-drift
   ii. Saw active service in the Second World War
b Four nationalities: Turkish German French Italian
   Two countries: Romania US
   One continent: Europe
c 1929 – the sleeping car was stuck in a snowdrift for 10 days.
d lunch / dinner / brunch / breakfast / afternoon tea

e i. bombed
   ii. shot at
   iii. marooned
   iv. stuck in a snow drift
f gleaming wood, polished brass, soft towels and crisp
  linen.
g In the dining car
   i. Lalique
   ii. Etoile du Nord
   iii. Chinoise
   iv. passengers' compartments.

D1 and D2 – various answers possible

D3 various answers possible

Hike up the mountain so that we can do the trip in our
own time
Spend a few days camping.
Have a look for the spectacled bear
See the other wildlife there
Have a look at the vegetation
Go on a train trip through the Sacred Valley
Take photographs without any tourists in them

Workbook answers

UNIT 17: What impact does fashion have on teenagers?

A1

A: The girl's hats are very beautiful.
B: The girls' hats are very beautiful.

A2

a I went to my sister-in-law's house.
b I went to my sisters-in-laws' houses.
c Mr Jones's shoes are too big for him.
d Monroe and Charles's house is in Zanzibar.
e It's a very hot day, so be careful of the sun.
f You should always dot your i's in a sentence.
g Children's clothes are on the first floor.
h This is my cousin's favourite uncle.

A3

a You can _detect_ if a person is lying by their heart rate.
b I prefer the original _version_ of the song.
c The suitcase is so _lightweight_ it won't be heavy to carry.
d She should be _monitored_ at all times until her temperature falls.
e These jeans are highly _wearable_ and washable.
f The milk and eggs should be _incorporated_ together in the cake mixture.
g The car is not only _aesthetically_ pleasing, but also an engineering miracle.
h _Civilian_ and military personnel are all invited to the grand opening.
i A thorn was _embedded_ in his foot and he couldn't walk.
j If you _improve_ your handwriting, I'll be able to read it!
k He was _diagnosed_ with diabetes when he was only 11!
l _Blending_ the two colours gives a softer shade.
m The sofa is made of _fabric_ and gets dirty easily.
n They could _generate_ more income by working more.

A4

a can be worn – wearable
b check something regularly – monitor
c cloth or material – fabric
d combine with – incorporate
e create – generate
f detect – recognise
g get better – improve
h identify an illness – diagnose

i mixing together – blending
j non-military – civilian
k placed inside – embedded
l specific variety – version
m weighing less than expected – lightweight
n appealingly – aesthetically

B1

a noun
b adverb
c adverb
d noun
e adjective
f adverb
g adverb
h verb

Adjective	Noun	Verb	Adverb
sociable	_society_	_socialise_	_socially_
permanent	_permanence_		_permanently_
wide	_width_	_widen_	_widely_
obscure	_obscurity_	_obscure_	_obscurely_
instantaneous	_instant_		_instantaneously_
mild			_mildly_
slight			_slightly_
ambitious	_ambition_		_ambitiously_

B3

Downloading tunes from the Internet <u>may</u> be a great new way to buy your music …

B4

It modifies the meaning of the main verb. Its function is 'possibility'

B5

a True
b True
c False
d True
e False
f True

B6

a I *should've* offered to babysit.

b I *ought* to help her across the road.

c I *must* study harder for this exam.

d *May* I open the window please? I'm so hot!

e I *can't* walk any more, I'm so tired.

f *Could* I borrow a pencil, please?

g My keys *might* be in my bag.

h I *will* be able to make it, but it's getting very late.

i Sorry, I *have* to leave now, as my bus leaves in ten minutes.

j I *will* cook if you do the washing up!

C1 and C2 – various answers possible

A1

was walking
a woman
turn left
car
no entry
animals not allowed
at a restaurant
the toilets
man
hospital
wheelchair
ramp
escalators
pushchairs
old people
at
post office
no smoking
hung up
a cup of tea
bed

A2

Across	Down
4. profound	1. language
5. expression	2. mature
7. fraction	3. option
8. dialect	4. pronunciation
9. statement	6. primary
10. rhythm	
11. ethnicity	

A3

a pronunciation
b profoundly
c option
d rhythm
e expression
f dialect
g primary

h ethnicity
i mature
j statement
k language
l fraction

B1

a The <u>black</u> window closed slowly. Attributive
b This stretch of river is very <u>dangerous</u>. Predicative
c Michael feels <u>ill</u>. Predicative
d A <u>larger</u> than necessary chocolate was given to the children. Attributive
e The <u>blue</u> sea is beautiful today. Attributive
f The man is <u>old</u>, but he's still able to be independent. Predicative

B2

a She had a <u>wonderful</u> smile when I greeted her.
b Her smile is <u>bright</u> and lights up her face.
c He bought two <u>large</u> bread rolls.
d She gave him a bucket of <u>dirty</u> water for the plants.
e He put his hand in the water – the water was very <u>hot</u>.
f They are a <u>close</u> family and do a lot together.
g The family appeared <u>exhausted</u> as they got off the train after their trip.
h I saw lots of <u>funny</u> clowns at the theatre that made me laugh.

B3

a You decide. It's up <u>to</u> you if you go.
b What <u>in</u> the world do you mean by that?
c Could you hold <u>on</u> a moment, please, while I change my shoes?
d He's got mixed feelings <u>about</u> his new college.
e Freeda feels very <u>strongly</u> about doing so much homework.
f She's so very pleased <u>with</u> her exam results.
g That <u>sounds</u> like a wonderful chance of a new experience.
h Thank you <u>so</u> much for inviting us to your house.

B4

a I'm good at learning languages, but <u>useless at</u> sciences.
b He <u>made</u> a mistake with his calculations in the maths exam.

c Can I <u>try</u> on this dress in size 12, please?
d Can I <u>assist</u> you, madam? No, thank you, I'm just looking .
e If you <u>ask</u> me, you should buy it today.
f If you don't mind me <u>saying</u> , that colour looks really nice on you.
g The way I <u>see</u> it, we've done all we can.
h You know <u>what</u> I think? She shouldn't go tonight.

C1 – suggested answers

literally – the exact meaning of something
fluid – liquid / flowing
constituent – essential
track – record
concepts – ideas
civilisations – people / society
papyrus - paper
elided – omitted
scribes – writers
scroll – document

C2

a civilisations
b literally
c concepts
d track
e papyrus
f scribes
g scroll
h fluid
i constituent
j elided

C3

a The formation of writing.
b They were limited and some things were difficult to depict.
c On lumps of wet clay.
d The Egyptian were more pictorial than the Sumerian, but both systems suggest objects and concepts
e Reserved for holy texts.
f It became easier.
g Needed a more abbreviated version from the pressure of business.

C4

Catwoman
Spider-Man
Thor
Batman
Wonder Woman
Superman
Iron Man
Incredible Hulk
Captain America
Black Widow

C5

a Superman
b Thor
c Iron Man
d Wonder Woman

C6

Superheroes became popular in the late 1930s and early 1940s.
Some of them are known internationally more than real historic figures.
Numerous television shows, books and movies have been published and produced about them.
Superman was the first comic book character.
Wonder Woman started life as a secretary.
Superheroes did lose out in popularity for a while in the 1950s.
Batman became popular again in 1966 when he came to television.
Superheroes now make mistakes and have some human qualities.
The 2012 Avengers film was one of the most financially successful.
Demand for Superhero paraphernalia has increased dramatically in recent years.
Superheroes have become much more sophisticated.

Acknowledgements

The author and publishers are grateful for the permissions granted to reproduce texts in either the original or adapted form. While every effort has been made, it has not always been possible to identify the sources of the all materials used, or to trace all copyright holders. If any omissions are brought to our notice, we will be happy to include the appropriate acknowledgements on reprinting.

pp. 6–7 adapted from www.nhm.ac.uk/about-us/news/2010/april/colossal-squid-joins-museum-tour64890.html, courtesy of the Natural History Museum; p. 12 adapted from www.weatherwizkids.com; pp. 16–17 adapted from National Geographic Image Collection, www.nationalgeographic.com, 2008; pp. 20–1 adapted with kind permission *Geography Homework Pack 1*, Pearson Publishing © 2000, www.pearsonpublishing.co.uk; p. 25 adapted from *The Kingfisher Facts and Records Book* (Kingfisher Publications, Pan Macmillan Publishing, 2000); p. 33 adapted from the Young People's Trust for the Environment website (www.ypte.org.uk); p. 38 adapted from http://www.nasa.gov/audience/foreducators/exploration-design-challenge-launch.html; p. 47 adapted from 'Survival Kit', *The Independent on Sunday*, 12th August 2007; p. 65 adapted from www.historyforkids.org/learn/clothing/index.htm, 2008, and from 'Ancient Clothing in Kidipede – History for Kids by Karen Carr, 2007; pp. 68–9 adapted from www.mania.com.

An environmentally friendly book printed and bound in England by www.printondemand-worldwide.com

PEFC Certified

This product is
from sustainably
managed forests
and controlled
sources

www.pefc.org

PEFC/16-33-415

This book is made of chain-of-custody materials; FSC materials for the cover and PEFC materials for the text pages.